General editor: Graham Handley MA PhD

Brodie's Notes on Jane Austen's

EMMA

Graham Handley MA PhD
Formerly Principal Lecturer and Head of English Department, The College of All Saints, Tottenham

Pan Books London, Sydney and Auckland

First published 1986 by Pan Books Ltd
Cavaye Place, London SW10 9PG
19 18 17 16 15
© Pan Books Ltd 1986
ISBN 0 330 50220 4
Photoset by Parker Typesetting Service, Leicester
Printed and bound in Great Britain by
Richard Clay Ltd, Bungay, Suffolk

Contents

Page references in these notes are to the Pan Classics edition of *Emma* but as references are also given to particular chapters, the Notes may be used with any edition of the novel.

Preface

The intention throughout this study aid is to stimulate and guide, to encourage the reader's *involvement* in the text, to develop disciplined critical responses and a sure understanding of the main details in the chosen text.

Brodie's Notes provide a summary of the plot of the play or novel followed by act, scene or chapter summaries each of which will have an accompanying critical commentary designed to underline the most important literary and factual details. Textual notes will be explanatory or critical (sometimes both), defining what is difficult or obscure on the one hand, or stressing points of character, style or plot on the other. Revision questions will be set on each act or group of chapters to test the student's careful application to the text of the prescribed book.

The second section of each of these study aids will consist of a critical examination of the author's art. This will cover such major elements as characterization, style, structure, setting, theme(s) or any other aspect of the book which the editor considers needs close study. The paramount aim is to send the student back to the text. Each study aid will include a series of general questions which require a detailed knowledge of the set book; the first of these questions will have notes by the editor of what *might* be included in a written answer. A short list of books considered useful as background reading for the student will be provided at the end.

Graham Handley

Literary terms as used in these notes

Jane Austen uses little **imagery**, but occasionally you will find a **metaphor**. This is a comparison which does not employ the introductory 'like' or 'as', whereas a **simile** uses one of these two words.

Irony runs throughout *Emma*. It consists of the humorous or sarcastic use of words to imply the opposite of what they commonly mean. But in Jane Austen the irony is not merely verbal. It relates to circumstances or situations, showing the incongruity between what is expected and what actually is. The whole of Emma's plans for Harriet and Mr Elton is seen *ironically*, since what *appears* (to Emma) is that Elton loves Harriet, but what actually *is* is that Elton loves Emma, who is completely unaware of it.

Dramatic irony, used effectively in plays, is employed here by Jane Austen; this is where the reader knows or suspects what characters do not know (in *Emma* the reader certainly suspects that Frank Churchill is interested in Jane Fairfax, but Emma and the Westons, for example, do not know this).

An **epigram** is a witty remark, often satirical, concisely expressed. Sometimes it is in the form of a **paradox**, where a seemingly absurd statement may prove to be true on close examination, or where what appears to be a contradiction is in fact true.

Antithesis is where a contrast of opposites is used (as in Pope's 'To err is human, to forgive, divine') and Jane Austen makes much use of this kind of balancing statement.

Tautology Saying the same thing twice over in different words, a serious fault in style, or indicative of character, as in Mrs Elton.

The author and her work

Jane Austen was born in December 1775 at Steventon in Hampshire where her father George Austen was Rector. Here she spent her childhood and young womanhood. Her father, who was later to recognize his daughter's unquestionable talents, took pupils and prepared them for Oxford, where two of his sons were to study. Jane's mother was a keen gardener, had a strong sense of humour, and suffered from lengthy bouts of ill-health. The Austens were a close family. The eldest son James had a curacy, and later succeeded his father at Steventon. While still a boy, the next brother Edward was adopted and brought up by well-to-do cousins at Godmersham in Kent. Henry, next in age, was certainly close to Jane in terms of sympathy, sharing her delightful sense of humour and particularly her wit. But closest of all to Jane was her sister Cassandra; their intimacy allowed her to mock her sister's talents while at the same time appreciating them – 'You are indeed the finest comic writer of the present age', she once wrote to her.

Jane's two other brothers Charles and Frank entered the Navy, where both achieved high rank. Jane was encouraged to write, her father even corresponding with a publisher on her account, and she often read aloud, particularly her early burlesques, to Cassandra. They were an engaging, attractive and largely unquarrelsome family. After their father's death, all the sons helped to support their mother. In 1782 Jane and Cassandra were sent to stay at a school in Reading, returning after about two years; by this time James was at Oxford. Their father's sister, who married a Frenchman, later became strongly attached to the Austens at Steventon. Her husband was executed in 1794 at the height of the French Revolutionary terror; it was probably through her that Jane learned much of the world outside Steventon.

In these impressionable years Jane Austen was certainly reading Dr Samuel Johnson (1709–84), Oliver Goldsmith (?1730–74), George Crabbe (1754–1832) and William Cowper (1731–1800) and a number of travel books. Most important of all she read all the novels she could lay her hands on. These were many and various. She began to write burlesques and parodies of many of her contemporary writers, almost anticipating Thackeray's published experiments in this vein some sixty years later. Obviously she wrote much before she was sixteen years old, and her juvenilia have been published with editorial commentaries in *Volume the First*, the *Second* and *Third*. The second volume is *Love and Freindship* (her spelling), in part told in letters, the form Jane inherited from the great 18th-century novelist Samuel Richardson, and also from other writers who employed the epistolary style.

There is some evidence that *Elinor and Marianne* was written in this style before 1796; it was later redrafted as *Sense and Sensibility*. *Lady Susan* was also composed in the form of letters, while *First Impressions* was finished in 1797 and offered by Mr Austen to the London publisher Cadell, who turned it down. The family had enjoyed it; it was later to be redrafted and published as *Pride and Prejudice*. By 1798 Jane Austen was well on with a novel which was to undergo heavy revisions before it emerged as *Northanger Abbey*.

Mr and Mrs Austen were bent on retiring to Bath, and the family certainly visited Ramsgate and Lyme Regis; Lyme was the location of the memorable scene in *Persuasion* where Louisa Musgrove falls off the Cobb and is injured. The Austens settled in Bath just after the turn of the century, and Jane is thought to have had an unhappy love affair at about this time. Jane never really liked Bath. By 1803 she had revised the early version of *Northanger Abbey*, though it had to wait for a number of years before being published.

The fragment of *The Watsons* was begun in 1803. In the following year Jane suffered the loss of her great friend Mrs Lefroy and at the beginning of 1805 her father died. During this period she was certainly depressed. In addition to family burdens, it must be remembered that she had received virtually no recognition as an author outside her own family. Her letters through this period still reflect her interest in people and how acutely she was sketching them. She wrote how thankful she was to leave for Clifton ('with what happy feelings of Escape'). This was in 1806, and in 1807 the family removed to Southampton, where they were to remain for the next three years. They became more intimate with Edward living at Godmersham, and when his wife died leaving eleven children, Jane and Cassandra found themselves constantly employed as aunts to this band of nephews and nieces.

By 1809 Jane was again in touch with her publisher over *Susan* (later *Northanger Abbey*), but although he was prepared to let her have back her copy for what he had paid for it, he put a bar on her publishing it. In 1809 she moved with her mother and sister to Chawton in Hampshire, and she still found herself happily in communication with a number of the younger members of her family. Some of these have left sympathetic and affectionate pictures of their aunt, who was generally content with her life at Chawton.

Early in 1811 *Sense and Sensibility* was published, and Jane was already revising *Pride and Prejudice*. This appeared in 1813, and when she received her own copy from London she wrote to Cassandra, 'I have got my own darling child.' As she has told us, she loved the character of Elizabeth Bennet as she had created her. From this period onwards her letters reflect how concerned she was with her own writing. She wrote, as we know, in the sitting-room, and it is apparent that *Sense and Sensibility*, *Pride and Prejudice* and *Mansfield Park* were being dealt with at revision or proof level at about the same time. Her works were published anonymously and, according to her brother Henry, she held back with each book 'till time and many perusals had satisfied her that the charm of recent composition was dissolved.'

Mansfield Park appeared in 1814, and was followed in 1815 by *Emma.* The latter received a generous review from Sir Walter Scott as well as the accolade from the Prince Regent's librarian J. S. Clarke, granting Jane Austen permission to dedicate any future work to the Prince Regent. He even went on to suggest that she might like to write 'an historical romance, illustrative of the august House of Coburg'. But her horizons, though narrower in terms of geographical and historical compass, were wide in inner human understanding. Henry retrieved the copyright of *Northanger Abbey*, and in 1816 Jane drafted the 'Advertisement' for the novel. This was printed – posthumously – with the text. But at this time she was busy with another novel, for she had begun *Persuasion*; she finished it in July 1816, though she cancelled one chapter which was virtually redrafted. This novel and *Northanger Abbey* were put aside while work on *Sanditon* was begun in January 1817. By March of that year she was very ill; in May she went to Winchester with Cassandra for medical attention. It was of no avail, and on 18 July she died, leaving *Northanger Abbey* and *Persuasion* to be published in the following year.

Thus lived and died in unremarkable and retired obscurity one of the greatest English novelists. Throughout her writings her moral stance is clear, uncompromising in its perspective, never sententious or smug. She invested the English novel with a new status, preparing the way for the great writers of the nineteenth century, like Charles Dickens (1812–70), George Eliot (1819–80) and Thomas Hardy (1840–1928). It has been said that her canvas was narrow, and there is no doubt that she would have been the first to have acknowledged this; such great events of her time as the French Revolution and the ensuing wars, excesses, idealisms and struggles find no place in her work. But her range encompassed the novelist's essential material; the affairs of the human heart. With refinement of style and a meticulous observation of character in action and interaction she brought to fictional characters a closer and deeper scrutiny than anything attempted in novels before.

Jane Austen learned much from her predecessors, but she imposed on the novel her own compactness of form, giving to her characters a consistent psychology and development that was to influence not only 19th-century novelists but those who were to write from the consciousness of character in the twentieth. Those who feel that her writings are those of an old maid should ask themselves if sexual passion has ever been depicted so strongly – not indulgently, not salaciously, not sensationally – as in the feelings of Darcy for Elizabeth Bennet. The conventions within which Jane lived demanded a certain code of conduct, an acceptance of what must not be uttered or seen; reticence ruled, yet her awareness encompasses all. We know that she knows, and that she intends us to know, that the gloss of polite conversation cannot hide people's basic motives. Her way is to be ironic without being cruel, satirical without being complacent, wide without being pretentious and, above all, human and understanding in her attitude towards the human condition. The purity and accuracy of her dialogue stand the test of time; to translate her to film, stage or television is not to translate but merely to accept – script-writers cannot improve her.

Jane's spirit is in many ways a comic one, and we might here recall Meredith's words in his *Essay on Comedy* that 'The laughter of Comedy is impersonal and of unrivalled politeness.' Her country house, parsonage and Bath society seem unaware of tragedy, the tragedy behind the teacups, the incest behind the domestic ritual which informs the novels of Ivy Compton-Burnett, for example. For Jane Austen's faith leads her to show us life as it generally is; she steers between the extremes of vinegar and saccharine by the simple expedient of being true to her eye and her ear; they never let her down.

Plot, chronology and setting

Plot

Emma Woodhouse, 'handsome, clever, and rich', has reached the age of twenty-one and is living with her father at Hartfield in the parish of Highbury. Emma is the younger of two sisters, their mother having died when they were children. Her sister Isabella is married before the novel begins to Mr John Knightley, and Emma has just lost her governess and inseparable companion, Miss Taylor, who has married Mr Weston. She leaves Hartfield and settles at nearby Randalls, with the result that Emma, who has been allowed to have her own way too much and is somewhat spoiled, is thrown upon her own resources. She is proud of having made the match between Mr Weston and Miss Taylor, but is gently reproved by her much respected neighbour Mr Knightley for indulging her inclination.

Harriet Smith, a girl of unknown parentage and educated at Mrs Goddard's school nearby, comes to one of Mr Woodhouse's evening card parties. There she is taken over by Emma, who introduces her into local society, and determines that Harriet will marry Mr Elton, the new vicar of Highbury. Meanwhile Harriet receives a proposal of marriage from Robert Martin, a local farmer. Though it is obvious that Harriet is greatly attracted to this young man, Emma cleverly persuades her to reject the proposal, considering Mr Martin not good enough to move in her (and now Harriet's) society. When Mr Knightley learns this he is angry with Emma who, however – while generally respecting his views – considers that he is wrong in this instance.

At Christmas the John Knightleys come to Hartfield and a party is held at Randalls. Harriet has a cold and cannot attend and Emma, who had thought that Mr Elton was paying marked attentions to Harriet before this, now finds to her embarrassment that she herself is the object of his love. He proposes to her; Emma realizes that she has misinterpreted his motives and is angry with him and with herself. She comforts Harriet in her suffering over this loss; Mr Elton recovers quickly and goes away for a time, returning as the fiancé of a Bristol woman Miss Hawkins. He later marries her and brings her to Highbury. She turns out to be a pretentious and vulgar woman.

Among the other residents of Highbury there is a garrulous spinster Miss Bates, living with her mother and, at this time, her niece Jane Fairfax. Jane has been staying with a family called Campbell, acting as companion to their daughter and finishing her own education. Miss Campbell marries a Mr Dixon, and Jane (now aged nineteen) returns to Highbury prior to taking up a post as a governess. She is accomplished and beautiful but somewhat cold and reserved and often in poor health. Emma admires her but cannot warm towards her. Meanwhile we hear much of a Mr Frank Churchill. He is the son of Mr Weston by his first wife. He was adopted by his uncle and aunt, the Churchills, with whom he has been staying. We later learn that he has met Jane Fairfax while on holiday at Weymouth, and when he arrives at Highbury Emma finds him a charming and attractive young man. She is, however, though appreciative of his attentions, determined not to marry, but to continue to live with her father. She gets some pleasure from the fact that she feels Frank may be in love with her and that the village is aware of their 'romance'. The Westons arrange to give a ball at the Crown Inn, but Frank is summoned back to Enscombe because of Mrs Churchill's illness. Frank says goodbye to Emma, who feels that he might have proposed and also that she is a little in love with him.

Mrs Elton now begins to exert her vulgar and insensitive influence. She patronizes Emma (hitherto the first lady of Highbury); is contemptuous of and rude to Harriet; and 'takes up' Jane Fairfax, being determined to find a suitable position for her. With the return of Frank the postponed ball is held at the Crown. Mr Elton slights Harriet by refusing to dance with her but, to Emma's delight, Mr Knightley, generally not a dancing man, comes to the rescue as partner for Harriet. This incident is followed by a dramatic one. Harriet and a friend are out walking when they encounter some gipsies; the friend runs away, and Harriet, surrounded by a threatening group, is rescued by Frank Churchill, thus giving rise to Emma's suspicion that perhaps Frank has an inclination towards her protegée. Her suspicions are fuelled when Harriet says that she loves someone far superior to Mr Elton.

Mr Knightley dislikes Frank Churchill, and tells Emma that he believes Frank is making advances both to her (Emma) and to

Jane Fairfax. Emma, though she has cooled towards Frank, laughs at this idea. A strawberry-picking outing is held at Donwell Abbey, Mr Knightley's home. Here Mrs Elton tells Jane that she has found a suitable post for her, but Jane says that she is not ready to accept it. Frank is all the time expected to arrive from Richmond to join this party; he is very late and, when he does arrive, is hot and irritable. Jane, meanwhile, in some distress has left the party and set out for home. The next day there is a picnic at the beauty spot of Box Hill. Frank flirts with Emma, the Eltons are rude and Emma, in an unguarded moment, is rude to Miss Bates. For this she is reproved by Mr Knightley and, realizing her error, she goes next day to apologize to Miss Bates. She learns that Jane is prostrated by a bad headache, and also that she has accepted the post which Mrs Elton had obtained for her. Frank, meanwhile, has returned to Richmond sooner than expected.

The news that Mrs Churchill is dead is followed swiftly by the revelation that Frank Churchill and Jane Fairfax have been secretly engaged for eight months. Emma is surprised – Frank's advances to her were a cover for his feelings for Jane Fairfax – but worried on account of Harriet. She thinks that the latter is in love with Frank, but when she tells her the news she is amazed to discover that the object of Harriet's affections is Mr Knightley. With this revelation Emma soon realizes the state of her own heart and gloomily contemplates the future: Mrs Weston is expecting a baby; Frank and Jane will leave the district; Knightley will marry Harriet. But he doesn't. His own feelings too have been well concealed. He proposes to Emma and she is glad to accept him.

The last phase of the plot is the rounding off into a happy ending for everyone. Frank has the decency to write a long letter of apology and explanation in which he stresses how he covered his feelings by flirting with Emma. As long as Mrs Churchill lived, he knew that his engagement to Jane would have to be secret; now he has his father's permission to marry her. Harriet returns to her former love Robert Martin (this time with Emma's approval and relief) and Emma has to contrive how best to soothe her father over her marriage. Fate intervenes in the form of some robberies in the village, and Mr Woodhouse is so worried by these that he agrees to the marriage and will doubtless feel secure under the protection of his son-in-law.

Chronology

Emma was written in 1814, and it is reasonable to suppose that it is set roughly at this time, though Frank Churchill's plan to travel abroad would seem to suggest a time of peace not war. This need not be taken too seriously, however. The action occupies roughly one year. Frank Churchill writes a letter to his father congratulating him on his marriage on *28 September*. *October* and *November* evenings are mentioned very near the beginning of the novel, and it is the *middle of December* when Emma, pushing Harriet into Mr Elton's way, contrives to get them both into the Vicarage because, she says, she has broken the lace of her boot. There is a mention of *January* in the New Year, and Frank Churchill comes to Highbury on his visit to the Westons in *February*. He stays for two weeks, but obtains the extension of a few days beyond this.

Emma pays her first visit to Mrs Elton in *March*, since she refers to her last visit to the Vicarage 'three months ago'. By *April* Mrs Elton is badgering Jane about a situation, and the Churchills rent their house in Richmond for *May* and *June*. It is 'almost Midsummer' when the visit to see the strawberry beds at Donwell is made, and to be exact it is 23 June. The trip to Box Hill is made the next day, and in the evening Frank goes back to Richmond. Within two days of his return Mrs Churchill dies. Early in *July* Frank comes to Randalls to reveal his secret engagement to Jane Fairfax. Two days later Emma reads Frank's letter, as does Knightley, and the next day Emma visits Jane. The marriages of the three couples are clearly set out – Harriet and Robert Martin in *September*, Emma and Knightley in *October*, Jane and Frank in *November*.

Setting

The action of the novel takes place in the large village of Highbury in the county of Surrey. Although Highbury has been identified with various places such as Cobham and Leatherhead, it is obviously an imaginary parish since, as R. W. Chapman has pointed out, no real place is at once 16 miles from London, 9 from Richmond and 7 from Box Hill. Jane Austen gives us an intimate picture of village life as led by the daughter of a country gentleman near the beginning of the nineteenth century. There are a number of attractive houses in the village, where the

Woodhouses are pre-eminent in status. The Woodhouses own the small estate of Hartfield while Mr Knightley their neighbour owns the rest of the nearby land and Donwell Abbey. Mr Weston, who marries Emma's governess-companion Miss Taylor, has made his money in trade and has acquired enough to buy Randalls, a small estate adjoining Highbury.

The village inn, the Crown, is of a moderate size. It keeps a couple of pairs of post-horses which are used for the local runs. The most patronized shop is Ford's, 'the principal woollen-draper, linen-draper and haberdasher's shop united', visited by most people every day, according to Mr Weston. In Chapter 27 we get a view of the busiest part of the village through Emma's eyes as she stands looking out from the door of this shop. She sees

Mr Perry walking hastily by, Mr William Cox letting himself in at the office-door, Mr Cole's carriage horses returning from exercise, or a stray letter-boy on an obstinate mule, were the liveliest objects she could presume to expect; and when her eyes fell only on the butcher with his tray, a tidy old woman travelling homewards from shop with her full basket, two curs quarrelling over a dirty bone, and a string of dawdling children round the baker's little bow-window eyeing the gingerbread, she knew she had no reason to complain.

Compare the tone of this with the description in Chapter 42 of a view from the garden of Donwell Abbey:

The considerable slope, at nearly the foot of which the Abbey stood, gradually acquired a steeper form beyond its grounds; and at half a mile distant was a bank of considerable abruptness and grandeur, well clothed with wood; – and at the bottom of this bank, favourably placed and sheltered, rose the Abbey-Mill Farm, with meadows in front, and the river making a close and handsome curve around it.

It was a sweet view – sweet to the eye and the mind. English verdure, English culture, English comfort, seen under a sun bright, without being oppressive.

The above two extracts are typical of Jane Austen's art – the eye for commonplace detail on the one hand, the scenic eye on the other – with a gloss on both which is redolent of wisdom and humanity.

The external settings are neatly balanced by what we may call the internal settings – the domestic life of the characters and those they employ. Emma has her own maid, the domestic arrangements of the house are under the supervision of the butler Serle, and James is in charge of the stables. The John Knightleys have a 'competent' number of nursery maids for their children. Dinner was taken regularly at four o'clock, and after dinner the ladies retired to the drawing-room while the men conversed over the wine and later joined the ladies for tea. There was a substantial supper later in the evening. Then Mr Woodhouse contents himself with a basin of thin gruel, while his guests have baked apples and biscuits, and a fricassee of sweet-bread and asparagus. Obviously conversation bulked large in these domestic settings; there were formal dinner parties and informal visits; and card playing was most popular. We are told that there was 'scarcely an evening in the week in which Emma could not make up a card-table for him', thus indicating that this was Mr Woodhouse's chief recreation apart from his hypo-chondria. There is a whist club in the village which is attended by Mr Elton and Mr Perry, while Mr John Knightley observes that Mr Weston plays whist five times a week with his neigh-bours. Musical evenings are also popular: Emma and Jane play the piano to their guests; there is often much singing; Mrs Elton tries to persuade Emma to help her start a music club.

That this setting is typical of its time among the leisured classes there is little doubt, and we note incidents in *Emma* that involved painting and drawing – Emma herself has always dab-bled. Sketching, its effects, and Mr Elton's going to London to get the frame, make an important contribution to the plot and the sequence of misunderstandings that Emma herself sets in train. Much space is also given in the novel to riddles and charades, both subserving the plot, while the children's alphabet provides Frank, Emma and Jane with the kind of interaction that is distasteful to the watching Mr Knightley. Dancing is not so common in Highbury as Frank Churchill had expected, but there is an informal dance after the Coles' dinner party and of course the formal ball at the Crown. Out-of-doors recreation consists of country walks and drives, and riding for the men. Seaside holidays are enjoyed by the John Knightley family and also by Frank Churchill, who goes sailing at Weymouth and meets the Campbells there and, most importantly, Jane Fairfax.

Most of the richer people have a carriage and horses, and use it to visit each other and to go for picnics. Mr Suckling's barouche-landau is an incontestable status symbol as far as Mrs Elton is concerned. Journeys to London are made on horseback by Mr Knightley and Frank Churchill. There seems to have been something of a horror of sleeping at inns among this class of people. When Mrs Churchill travels from Enscombe to London (about 190 miles) she is in such a hurry to arrive that she spends only two nights on the road. Both Mr Woodhouse and Mrs Elton mention the dirty and draughty condition of inns.

Educational settings are used in pivotal contrast in *Emma*. Notice this ironic account of education and what passes for it, in Chapter 3:

Mrs Goddard was the mistress of a school – not of a seminary, or an establishment, or any thing which professed, in long sentences of refined nonsense, to combine liberal acquirements with elegant morality upon new principles and new systems – and where young ladies for enormous pay might be screwed out of health and into vanity – but a real, honest, old-fashioned Boarding-school, where a reasonable quantity of accomplishments were sold at a reasonable price, and where girls might be sent to be out of the way and scramble themselves into a little education, without any danger of coming back prodigies.

This is complemented by the contrasting pictures of a governess's life. Miss Taylor led a happy life with the Woodhouses as one of the family. She is a greatly treasured and much missed companion. But when Jane seeks a similar post the author speaks of her decision to 'retire from all the pleasures of life, of rational intercourse, equal society, peace and hope, to penance and mortification for ever'. It is a bleak picture, and despite Mrs Elton's interest on Jane's account we can't help feeling that Jane would have been treated as a menial among menials.

The settings of *Emma* provide a keen insight into the everyday lives and habits of a section of English life, and the novel gives us the flavour of authentic social history of the time, albeit limited to one area, that of the middle-class country gentry.

Chapter summaries, critical commentaries, textual notes and revision questions

Emma Woodhouse, 'handsome, clever and rich' and aged twenty-one, lives with her father at Highbury in Surrey. Her governess of sixteen years, Miss Taylor, has just married Mr Weston and has gone to live at Randalls, a nearby estate. After the wedding Emma and her father discuss the 'loss' of Miss Taylor and Emma is hard put to know how she will bear it. Mr Woodhouse refers to 'poor Miss Taylor' and plays backgammon. Both are pleased when their neighbour, Emma's brother-in-law Mr Knightley, appears bringing them news of Isabella, Emma's sister and her children, whose home in London he has been visiting. After some banter about the wedding, including Emma's own claim that she herself made Miss Taylor's marriage for her some four years ago, Mr Knightley reproves Emma for her interference. Undeterred, she determines to bring her match-making powers to bear again, this time with the object of finding a wife for Mr Elton, the new Vicar of Highbury.

Commentary

This first chapter underlines with considerable irony Emma's nature – she is spoiled, self-willed, used to getting her own way – 'highly esteeming Miss Taylor's judgement, but directed chiefly by her own' (p.19). She is also somewhat conceited, but her valuation of Miss Taylor shows that she is warm-hearted and sentimental too. She is also devoted to her father, though there is every indication that he tries her patience considerably. There is more delightful irony: in the fact that Miss Taylor is only going to be half a mile away from them anyway; also at the expense of Mr Woodhouse himself obsessed by his health. The chapter sets the scene, describes Highbury 'The Woodhouses were first in consequence there') and contains some delightful dialogue as Mr Woodhouse complains where we would normally expect celebration. The dialogue, as always in Jane Austen, rings true to life. Mr Woodhouse's concern for Knightley gives way to that gentleman's common sense and his own satirical tone about the wedding ('Who cried most?'). The give-and-take humour of the relationship between Emma and Knightley immediately becomes apparent, but we notice the considered stress on Emma's capacity for match-making and Knightley's disapproval of it, a moral notation of a fault in Emma which she will not acknowledge. Emma is nothing if not obstinate.

them Notice how italics are used, here to imply intimacy, but for emphasis from time to time in the novel.
alloy To spoil, mar.
unexceptionable i.e. reliable, normal, *not* extraordinary.
attach i.e. her attentions.
valetudinarian One who is constantly concerned with his own ailments, imagined or real.
Hartfield . . . Highbury The first the part of the village, the second the village itself, about 16 miles from London.
in lieu Instead.
backgammon Played on a double board with draughts and dice.
Brunswick-square Just over a mile from St Paul's Cathedral, London, a fashionable area.
mizzle Drizzle.

Chapter 2

The chapter opens with a retrospect on Mr Weston. He had been born in Highbury, joined the militia, become a Captain, and married Miss Churchill, a Yorkshire heiress whose family disowned her on her marriage. They lived unhappily beyond their income, and after three years the wife died. Their son Frank was adopted by the Churchills, and Mr Weston left the militia and entered trade. Over the twenty-year period referred to he made a small fortune, bought an estate near Highbury, and married Miss Taylor. His son Frank (who has taken the name of Churchill) writes to Miss Taylor after the marriage, and Highbury extols the letter and expects a visit from him. Mr Woodhouse continues to pity 'poor Miss Taylor' but as the weeks pass is relieved that at least all the wedding-cake, that highly-indigestible substance, has all gone.

Commentary

The retrospect on Mr Weston touches on one of the themes of the novel, that of snobbery; the class differences are also stressed, and we note that the miniature of the first Mrs Weston is not unlike the condescending full-size portrait of Mrs Elton to come. Note the directness of Jane Austen's writing; she covers a number of years in a few paragraphs. There is an insight into the sound good sense and warmth of Mr Weston, some focus too on the hard work which brings its own reward in his achievements. Narrative expectation in Frank Churchill is aroused through the letter and the delightful gossip about it. Mrs Weston is sensitive to her new situation, her relationship to this young man and her past with Emma. The chapter ends with the joke of Mr Perry's children being seen eating wedding-cake; obviously the cake had been taken and distributed because of Mr Woodhouse's fear of its injurious effects!

a small independence i.e. an inheritance.
militia A county force commanded by the Lord Lieutenant of the county, the officers being men of some position.
embodied i.e. in service.
decorum i.e. show of manners (here used ironically).
Enscombe In Yorkshire (fictitious place name).
easy competence Sufficient income.
portionless i.e. lacking a dowry on marriage.
apprehension Idea.
ennui Boredom.
apothecary One licensed to prescribe drugs.

Chapter 3

Mr Woodhouse enjoys card parties with his friends and neighbours in the evenings; the Westons, Mr Knightley and Mr Elton the vicar are among his regular guests. Among the 'second set' are Mrs and Miss Bates, the former the widow of a vicar of Highbury, and Mrs Goddard, 'the mistress of a School'. Mrs Goddard requests that she may bring her 'parlour-boarder' Miss Harriet Smith to one of the parties. Emma is delighted; Harriet, of unknown birth, is 'a very pretty girl' and she is almost immediately taken over by Emma, who determines to make something of her by detaching her from her former friends and establishing her in good society. Mr Woodhouse continues to talk his way through the health risks of his guests by advising them on what to eat; Harriet, meanwhile, is delighted by the 'affability' of the equally delighted Emma.

Commentary

This is a scene-setting chapter with an important plot development; it brings together the main elements of Highbury society
at Mr Woodhouse's evening card parties, and it provides Emma
with a new impulse towards match-making and social education
in the person of Harriet Smith. Quite simply, the latter fills
Emma's psychological need to have someone whom she can
mould now that Miss Taylor has married. There is an account of
characters who are to play some part in the narrative, and
particularly of the talkative but essentially good Miss Bates. Mrs
Goddard's school affords the author the opportunity to condemn those educational establishments where 'young ladies for
enormous pay might be screwed out of health and into vanity'
(p.31). Note Emma's snobbery with regard to Harriet Smith's
friends and the authorial irony which embraces Emma's
schemes and her father's talk. It is a neat contrast – the first
perhaps harmful, the second trivial and harmless.

come-at-able i.e. available.
quadrille A card-game for four people.
quick-sighted Immediately appreciative.
mine of felicity Embodiment of truth.
seminary School.
long sentences of refined nonsense Note Jane Austen's satirical verve
  about this aspect of unwarranted advertising.
prosings i.e. talk (almost certainly of a trivial nature).
natural daughter i.e. illegitimate.
parlour-boarder Boarding-school pupil who 'lived in' with the family
  of the mistress of the school.
scalloped oysters i.e. oysters baked in scallop shells.

Chapter 4

Emma is delighted to find that Harriet is nearly all that she
expected her to be; she finds out nothing about her birth but
quite a lot about her friends the Martins and of Harriet's stay
with them. She gets Harriet to talk more and more of the young
farmer Robert Martin, and realizes that Harriet is likely to be
caught by this family. She advises her against intimacy with
them. On the next day they meet Robert Martin – Emma finds
him plain – and compares his lack of gentlemanly qualities by
drawing parallels with Mr Knightley and Mr Weston. Harriet's

warmth towards him cools and Emma proceeds to praise Mr
Elton's qualities and to draw Harriet's attention to the fact that
he has praised her. She is determined to bring Harriet and Mr
Elton together.

Commentary

There is some pathos in Emma's need for a companion;
although the motive is a selfish one it humanizes her in our eyes.
Emma enjoys playing – indeed being – the patron, and also
condescending to Harriet, who is gullible, pliable and not exactly
gifted with understanding. She has one quality, however, and
that is warm naturalness in her response to the Martin family
and to the attentions of Robert Martin himself. She is essentially
a simple girl who delights in simple things like the 'very pretty
little Welch cow' (p.35). Her account of the Martins brings out
Emma's natural snobbery despite the family's obvious kindness –
Mrs Martin sending Mrs Goddard a goose; and Robert Martin's
obvious attachment – going three miles out of his way to find
Harriet some walnuts. The author adopts a satirical tone
towards Harriet's choice of reading, and Emma adopts a snobbish one towards comparative status – 'The yeomanry are precisely the order of people with whom I feel I can have nothing to
do' (p.37). She proceeds to overcome Harriet by the use of
uncompromising language – 'I wish you may not get into a
scrape ... people who would take pleasure in degrading you'
(p.38). After the meeting with Robert Martin Emma is able to
stress his plainness, his want of manner, and then to invoke the
comparisons she is sure will influence Harriet. This is social
blackmail, and we notice Emma's determination, her obstinacy,
her power of manipulation, her blindness to Harriet's needs and
the quality of Harriet's response to Robert Martin and the
family.

For Mrs Weston there was nothing to be done; for Harriet everything.
   Note the antithetical balance of this – a favourite Jane Austen stylistic
   device.
Alderneys A famous breed of cattle from the Channel Islands.
sink herself for ever Note the image, expressive of Emma's snobbery.
Elegant Extracts Selections compiled by Vicesimus Knox in 1789.
the Vicar of Wakefield The novel by Oliver Goldsmith published in
   1766.

Romance of the Forest . . . Children of the Abbey The first by Mrs
  Radcliffe published in 1791, the second by Maria Regina Roche in
  1796.
beforehand with the world i.e. enjoy his money before he has earned
  it.
insensible of manner i.e. ignorant of the right behaviour.
clownish i.e. peasant-like, boorish.
sufferable i.e. endurable, to be tolerated.
expediency Appropriateness.
efficacy Right result.

Chapter 5

Mr Knightley engages Mrs Weston in conversation about
Emma's friendship with Harriet Smith. He obviously feels that it
may do Harriet some harm, but Mrs Weston is all for it. Mr
Knightley reminds her that Emma rarely sees anything through,
and that she lacks patience and self-discipline. They both join in
praise of Emma, though, and Mrs Weston sticks to her point that
Emma's intimacy with Harriet is not doing either of them any
harm. Knightley shows his warm interest in Emma, and we
suspect that Mrs Weston too has romantic ideas about Emma's
future.

Commentary

Again we note the natural ease of the dialogue. We also learn
more about Emma, more particularly the fact that while vowing
to read much and drawing up lists she has never completed a
course of study. Knightley is ironic about her in a kindly way,
and reiterates that he considers she is spoilt. He stresses her
cleverness, but adds that 'Emma has been mistress of the house
and of you all' (p.43). It is quite obvious that Knightley and Mrs
Weston have real respect for each other. He continues to point
out what injuries Harriet may suffer by thinking Emma perfect
when in fact she is far from being so. Knightley allows, however,
that she is not vain, and reveals something of his own heart when
he says 'I have a very sincere interest in Emma' (p.45). Their
pondering on her lack of readiness for marriage and Emma's
own assertion that she will not marry provide us with an insight
into the Westons – perhaps they too are setting store by the visit
of Frank Churchill, which may change Emma's destiny!

wantonness Here the meaning is an over-supply, luxuriousness (not the more usual irresponsibility or licentiousness).
put her out of conceit i.e. spoil her view of.
spleen Mood, temper.
some doubt of a return i.e. in some doubt as to whether her love is returned.

Revision questions on Chapters 1–5

1 Write a character sketch of Emma as she has appeared so far.

2 What aspects of the novel do you find funny? Refer to specific incidents in your answer.

3 By a close analysis of any two conversations, show how Jane Austen is the mistress of natural dialogue.

4 Write an essay on Jane Austen's use of retrospect in these early chapters.

Chapter 6

Emma seems to be achieving what she wants in fostering Mr Elton's interest in Harriet. She fetches out a collection of half-finished portraits of her family, is suitably flattered by Mr Elton, and persuades Harriet to sit for her own portrait. Mr Elton bustles around throughout, defending Emma's skill as an artist against the criticism of Mr Knightley. Mr Woodhouse thinks the portrait of Harriet pretty, but is rather worried that Emma has set it out of doors, where he fears Harriet might catch cold. A frame is needed for the picture, and Mr Elton volunteers to go to London to get one. Emma is rather overcome by Mr Elton's gallantry, but concludes that 'He is an excellent young man, and will suit Harriet exactly' (p.52).

Commentary

Emma convinces herself that Mr Elton is well on the way to being in love with Harriet; this reveals her blindness. She is also deaf to Mr Elton's innuendo, which is directed at her and not at Harriet. Elton himself strikes one as over-flattering and insincere. The display of Emma's previous attempts at art show that facet of her character which Knightly has stressed – her inability to complete anything – but it also provides both Elton and Harriet with the opportunity to display their own uncritical adulation of Miss Woodhouse. In an unguarded remark about 'No husbands and wives' Emma gives Mr Elton fuel for hope. She cannot stop his flattery, however, and we welcome Knightley's criticism – he is honest, Elton sycophantic. Emma is, so far, a poor judge of character. There is a delightfully ironic moment when Mr Woodhouse speaks of Harriet's catching cold, and another failure on Emma's part to read Mr Elton's motivation when he volunteers to go to London to get the picture framed.

cockade Baby's bonnet.
pet Temper.
declaration i.e. of his love for Harriet.
complaisance ... unexceptionable Self-satisfaction ... natural.
incommoding Inconveniencing.
as a principal i.e. if I were the first in his heart (which of course she is).

Chapter 7

Harriet comes to Hartfield sooner than expected, and tells Emma forthwith that she has received a marriage proposal from Robert Martin. Emma reads the letter, finds it better than she expected but, realizing Harriet's dependence on her advice, gives it while affecting to let Harriet judge for herself. Initially Harriet had been rather pleased and was somewhat taken aback by the coolness of Emma's reaction, but she allows herself to be subtly influenced. When Harriet decides to refuse the proposal, Emma gives her own approval and points out that she, Emma, could not have visited Harriet if she had been the wife of a farmer. Emma helps Harriet write her answer; Harriet obviously feels for Robert Martin, but Emma manages to switch to the subject of Mr Elton.

Commentary

Note here the speed of the action, the directness with which Jane Austen conveys Robert Martin's proposal – perhaps reflecting the directness of Robert Martin's character. Note too how Harriet's reactions are effectively conveyed in direct speech. Emma refuses to allow her feelings to be influenced, despite the quality of the letter, which she acknowledges. Emma is devious enough to make her own views clear while professing neutrality, and unscrupulous enough to make the weight of her advice very strong indeed before the reply is given. When she reveals her own snobbery ('Harriet had not surmised her own danger') she reinforces it by the unnecessary and insensitive consideration of Robert Martin's conceit. Her writing of the letter in effect compounds the completeness of her influence. She quickly changes the conversation when Harriet, obviously concerned about the effect her letter will have on Robert Martin and her future relations with the family, displays a sensitivity to effects which Emma herself at this stage lacks. The chapter puts the seal on Emma's misguided interference.

collect Gather, consider.
Bond-street Then, as now, a fashionable quarter of the West End of London.

Chapter 8

After spending the night at Hartfield, Harriet returns to Mrs Goddard's the next morning. Mr Knightley calls; Mr Woodhouse leaves to take his walk; Knightley confides in Emma that Harriet is improved under her tutelage and that 'your little friend will soon hear of something to her advantage' (p.59). He tells her that Robert Martin wishes to marry Harriet, and Emma is able to reply that Robert Martin has already proposed and been rejected. In the ensuing angry exchange Knightley blames Emma for spoiling Harriet's chances. He considers the advantages of such a marriage all on Harriet's side, while Emma thinks Robert Martin Harriet's inferior. Knightley tells Emma that she is giving Harriet ideas above her station. Emma is unrepentant but, because she always respects Mr Knightley's judgement, is left uncomfortable by this exchange. He goes on to warn her that if she has designs on Mr Elton for Harriet, her efforts will be in vain since Elton would not make an indiscreet marriage. Emma says that she has finished with match-making and Mr Knightley departs abruptly, leaving Emma somewhat worried by his views on Elton, though she convinces herself that he is wrong. Harriet afterwards arrives with the news that Mr Elton has gone to London with the picture.

Commentary

There is the usual comedy attendant upon any decision of Mr Woodhouse's. Then Knightley's directness brings on an emotional confrontation between himself and Emma. Knightley is generous and genuine on Robert Martin's account; he is also intuitive on Emma's, for he says unequivocally 'You saw her answer! you wrote her answer too' (p.61). His anger is based on a common-sense and accurate appraisal; Emma's rejection of his arguments on misguided snobbery, the triviality of social distinctions. As Knightley puts it, Emma is 'abusing the reason you have' (p.63). Emma is not entirely free from the effects of conscience, but she is something of a barometer at this stage. She believes herself right, and the timely arrival of Harriet with the news of Elton's departure only confirms her own belief in the rightness of her judgement.

unexceptionable Entirely suitable.
asperity Sharpness of temper.
Waiving Setting aside.
Were you, yourself, ever to marry . . . A wonderful moment of irony. Emma is later to fear that Mr Knightley and Harriet are in love, and in the process she discovers her own feelings for Mr Knightley.
to catch at i.e. make do with (an inferior match).
errant Here the meaning is 'complete [nonsense]'. Another example of Jane Austen's eccentric spelling. (Usually, of course, written as 'arrant nonsense'.)
materially cast down i.e. completely depressed.

Chapter 9

Mr Knightley continues displeased with Emma, while she continues to match-make. When the picture has been returned in its elegant frame, she, Mr Elton and Harriet transcribe charades into an album. After displaying his modesty, Mr Elton invents one and gives it to Emma. She believes that it is meant for Harriet, though the latter cannot solve it without her mentor's help. When Emma tells her that the answer is 'courtship' and points out the significance of the riddle – that Mr Elton is in love with her, Harriet – Harriet is amazed at her own good fortune. The riddle is then explained to Mr Woodhouse. This is followed by a discussion of the coming visit of Mr and Mrs John Knightley – Mr Woodhouse has his apprehensions – and when Mr Elton visits them again Emma returns his charade.

Commentary

The opening words of the chapter show Emma's obstinacy of spirit: 'Mr Knightley might quarrel with her, but Emma could not quarrel with herself' (p.67). The focus on riddles and charades gives a good insight into the occupations of Emma's class at the time (note the irony which implies that this is much easier than studying). The further irony shows that Emma is easily fooled by Mr Elton's apparent delicacy in approaching *her* with the charade. The gap between Emma and Harriet in understanding the charade is also ironically explored, though there is some pathos in the way that Harriet is so completely influenced by Emma's views ('Whatever you say is always right', p.72). Harriet contributes her own mite of unconscious irony when she says 'You and Mr Elton are one as clever as the other' (p.73). Mr Woodhouse provides much of the comedy with his 'Kitty, a fair but frozen maid' (p.75), and his thoroughly selfish but acceptable possessiveness over the forthcoming visit of Isabella and the children.

quarto of hot-pressed paper A book of smooth and glossy paper.

cyphers and trophies Monograms and decorations.

'Kitty, a fair but frozen maid ...' From the *New Foundling Hospital For Wit*, Part Four (1771). The succeeding verses make it clear that the answer was 'A Chimney-Sweeper'.

Neptune The Roman God of the sea.

a motto to the chapter Novelists often placed quotations in the form of mottoes to their chapters – of Jane Austen's contemporaries the most prolific user of the motto was Sir Walter Scott (1771–1832).

The course of true love never did run smooth Shakespeare, *A Midsummer Night's Dream*, I,1,134.

Michaelmas One of the four Quarter Days, 29 September.

couplet Two rhyming lines.

refine i.e. ponder upon.

he rather pushed it towards me This should have given Emma the clue that it was *for her*.

Elegant Extracts 'Kitty, a fair but frozen maid' is not in this. See note above.

Garrick's David Garrick (1717–79) the famous actor/producer.

made a push ... thrown a die i.e. gambled, achieved something (by writing the charade).

effusion Outpouring in words.

Chapter 10

Emma and Harriet visit a sick and poor family, passing the Vicarage on the way. Harriet has never been inside. She discusses with Emma why the latter has never married. Emma tells her that she has never been in love and does not think that she will be. They also talk about Jane Fairfax, Miss Bates's niece, before proceeding to the cottage and comforting its inhabitants. On their way back they meet Mr Elton; Emma so contrives it that he walks ahead with Harriet. Emma then breaks her bootlace deliberately, and asks to call at the Vicarage in order to replace it. When they enter Harriet and Mr Elton are left alone for a while, and Emma is pleased with the progress of her schemes for them so far.

Commentary

There is light authorial irony in the reference to Mr Elton's 'blessed abode', with Emma prophesying Harriet's future occupation of it. We see how little Emma knows her real self in the talk of marriage; there is self-satisfaction (and pathos) in her description of her unmarried power, but also a lack of generosity about Miss Bates which anticipates her later rudeness to that lady. Emma's talk of her own future caring for her sister's children leads naturally to the introduction of Jane Fairfax into the conversation. Again Emma is quite outspoken about Miss Bates's constant talk about Jane, and gives an early indication of her own jealousy – 'I wish Jane Fairfax well; but she tires me to death' (p.81). Another human aspect of Emma is shown in her reaction to visiting the poor; she feels that the experience has done her good, but doesn't know how long she will retain the impression of it. Authorial irony ensures that it is not for long. The appearance of Mr Elton sees Emma using her native cunning to bring him and Harriet together, despite Harriet's dependence on her. Emma continues to be deceived as to Mr Elton's real intentions.

pollards Trees with their branches cut back to encourage growth.
And I am not only, not going to be married . . . Although Emma does marry, there is some pathos here. She always puts her responsibilities to her father first.
conceit i.e. sympathy.

stomacher An ornamental covering for the chest.
parley Talk.
Stilton cheese, the north Wiltshire The first a rich blue-veined cheese,
  made chiefly in Cambridgeshire and named after a coaching inn at
  Stilton, where it was sold to travellers; the second is like cheddar
  cheese, but made in Wiltshire.
pales Boundary fences.
The lovers were standing together . . . Note this wonderful irony –
  they are 'lovers' in Emma's eyes, and the observation is made from her
  consciousness.

Revision questions on Chapters 6–10

1 How far do you think Emma is justified in her belief that the
object of Mr Elton's attentions is Harriet?

2 Show how Emma influences Harriet in her response to
Mr Martin's proposal.

3 Write an essay indicating what you (a) admire and (b) dislike
in Emma's character as revealed in these chapters.

4 Write a character sketch of Harriet as she appears in these
chapters.

5 What qualities in Mr Knightley do you particularly respect
and why?

Chapter 11

With the arrival of Mr and Mrs John Knightley Emma decides
that Mr Elton 'must now be left to himself'. Husband and wife are
described in some detail, and there is no doubt that Isabella is like
her father in seeing the melancholy side of things. She shows this
immediately by her sympathy for his 'loss' of Miss Taylor, though
Emma points out that they see the Westons every day. The
conversation inevitably turns to the topic of Frank Churchill and
his kind letter to his stepmother, with the susceptible Mrs Knightley wondering how Mr Weston could ever have yielded up his son.

Commentary

The main interest of this chapter is centred on the visitors. They
form an interesting contrast. Jane Austen establishes a family

consistency by having Isabella recognizably like her father, but before that there is some delightful comedy at the expense of Mr Woodhouse and how everything is arranged so as not to discomfort him. Isabella is not gifted with great understanding (note the contrast with Emma) but her husband is intelligent, blunt, stands no nonsense, and consequently gives offence – though we are left in no doubt that his heart is in the right place. He displays a neat sense of humour about the 'loss' of Miss Taylor – he asks Emma 'whether there were any doubts of the air of Randalls' (p.87). He nearly offends Emma by implying that Mr Weston prefers society to family affection, and we note that Emma is capable of strong self-discipline on this occasion.

a competent number i.e. what was necessary.
quickness i.e. sharpness of insight.
out of humour Irritable, bad-tempered.
material Important, relevant.
Cobham A village on the River Mole in Surrey.

Chapter 12

Mr Knightley dines at Hartfield on the first day of his brother's visit, and makes up his quarrel with Emma. While the brothers discuss the running of the farm at Donwell, Mr Woodhouse bemoans to Isabella the fact that she has spent some time at Southend instead of visiting him. Emma acts as diplomat and peacemaker, adroitly switching the conversation to Mr Perry and Mrs and Miss Bates. She is only partly successful, since Mr Woodhouse, his obsession with health always present, talks with distaste of the unhealthiness of London, says that none of the John Knightleys look well, and reverts to South End and the visit. He has the lack of tact to cite Mr Perry on the unhealthiness of South End and the fact that Cromer is to be preferred; Mr John Knightley rises to this, suggesting that Mr Perry should mind his own business. Only the efforts of Knightley and Emma prevent open friction between Mr Woodhouse and his son-in-law.

Commentary

Mr Woodhouse's selfishness and Emma's need for reconciliation with Mr Knightley dominate the early part of this chapter. Emma is greatly humanized in the process. The Knightley

brothers show their practicality, though this is almost interrupted by Mr Woodhouse's feeling that they need gruel. His
constant reference to South End and the holiday spent away
from him shows how selfish and yet pathetically dependent he is.
Emma reveals how genuinely anxious she is to keep the peace,
and we are made more aware of the domestic strains upon her.
Mrs Knightley reveals herself to be good-natured, somewhat
sugary (note her praise of Jane Fairfax) and of the same tactlessly melancholy nature as her father; John Knightley becomes
angry at his father-in-law's criticism of him via Mr Perry, but
Knightley himself shows that he is capable of adopting the
Emma-role, and prevents a crisis.

conversible i.e. having pleasant talk.
South End (now Southend), resort 30 miles from London, just north of
  the Thames Estuary.
coddling Fussing unnecessarily.
will it answer? i.e. will it be good enough?
Philippics Denunciations, from the Philippics of the Greek orator
  Demosthenes denouncing Philip of Macedon.
Cromer On the Norfolk coast, 120 miles from London.

Chapter 13

Mr Weston arranges a dinner-party at Randalls for Christmas
Eve, and even Mr Woodhouse is persuaded to go. Harriet and
Mr Elton are also invited, but Harriet has developed a sore
throat and has to stay at Mrs Goddard's to be nursed. Emma
visits her and meets Mr Elton on his way there as well as Mr John
Knightley and his two sons. Emma, intent on her scheme, diplo-
matically advises Mr Elton that he need not attend the dinner-
party, but Mr Elton is quick to seize the offer of a seat in Mr
Knightley's carriage for the visit. When Mr Elton has left, Mr
John Knightley, having summed up Mr Elton pretty accurately,
warns Emma that Elton is on the way to being in love with her
and that she ought to 'regulate your behaviour accordingly'
(p.100). Emma is put out that her brother-in-law should speak so
to her and considers him completely mistaken.

  Throughout the journey to Randalls, and after it has begun to
snow, Mr John Knightley complains to Emma of their stupidity
in leaving their own fireside on such a night. They pick up Mr
Elton; he has heard that Harriet is rather worse. To Emma's

surprise and John Knightley's disgust Mr Elton is in good spirits at the prospect of dining out, and talks of the pleasures of the season.

Commentary

Emma continues on her misguided way, assuring Harriet how concerned Mr Elton will be about her illness. When she tells Mr Elton he is all concern – the irony being that he is solicitous that Emma will not catch the infection. Emma in her blindness almost persuades Mr Elton that he should not go to Randalls, but is forestalled by Mr John Knightley's offering him a seat in his carriage. Emma ponders Mr Elton's responses, but the down-to-earth John Knightley sees through the man at once, assuring Emma that she is the real object of his attentions. Emma here reveals her obstinacy, and John Knightley reveals something of his own nature when he objects to leaving his own fireside in such weather. He worries and frets, and obviously dislikes venturing into society. When they arrive Mr Elton's civilities bear out what John Knightley feels – that Elton's attentions are directed towards Emma rather than Harriet. Elton's shallowness is revealed, and he recalls with delight that 'I was snowed up at a friend's house once for a week. Nothing could be pleasanter' (p.102). Mr John Knightley becomes progressively more grim, Mr Elton more superficial, as they drive to Randalls.

a soft air i.e. a softening of expression betraying his interest in her.
the sweep-gate The gate into the curved drive in.

Chapter 14

The visit is paid and Emma, as always, is greatly cheered by Mrs Weston, though she finds that Mr Elton is always in her company. He appears happy and forgetful of Harriet, and Emma begins to sense that her brother-in-law's suspicions may be right. He (Elton) pays marked attention to Emma, but she is somewhat diverted by the mention of Frank Churchill. Mr Weston says that his son will pay them a visit if he can get away from Mr and Mrs Churchill at Enscombe in January. Mr Weston gives some account of the character of Mrs Churchill and of her possessive fondness for Frank, Mrs Weston stresses the fact that Mrs Churchill 'is a very odd-tempered woman', and confides to Emma that she feels the Churchills want to keep Frank to themselves because they are jealous. Emma ponders on the character of Mrs Churchill herself.

Commentary

Emma shows her genuine delight in the companionship of Mrs Weston, a reflection of her loyalty. The usual quiet irony plays over the discussion of Harriet's cold and Mr Woodhouse's narration of its history and other trivia. There is an incisive look into Emma's character as she feels – though only in passing – that Mr Elton is behaving 'like a would-be lover'. We note too her possessive thoughts about Frank Churchill even before she has met him (but remember her resolution not to be married) and her awareness (and perhaps conceit) in thinking that people will consider that she and Frank are a match. Mr Weston honestly acknowledges the Churchills' possessiveness over Frank, but has the generosity of spirit to appreciate Mrs Churchill's fondness for his son.

Chapter 15

The men join the ladies in the drawing-room, Mr Elton immediately expressing his anxiety for Emma, his fear that she will catch Harriet's infection. Emma is rather annoyed by this but just then Mr John Knightley comes in to announce that the ground is covered with snow. He takes some mild joy in teasing Mr Woodhouse about the state of the roads, suggesting they may be impassable, but Mr Weston allays anxieties about this. Isabella panics and wants the carriage ordered immediately before the weather gets worse, but Knightley has been outside to inspect the conditions and reassures them. Because of Mr Woodhouse's own fears, however, the carriages are sent for and Emma finds herself closeted with Mr Elton in one of them. They are hardly out of the gate before he tells her that he loves her. Emma is horrified, and cites his interest in Harriet. He is quick to disown this and to assert that he is only interested in Emma herself. He tells her that she has encouraged him. Emma's anger mounts on her own and Harriet's account, and Elton in his turn is angered into silence by her rejection of him. Emma is relieved when the journey ends.

Commentary

This superb chapter shows how Emma's judgement has been completely astray with regard to Mr Elton. In a sense she gets what she deserves. Emma and Mr Elton alone in the carriage provide a dramatic and claustrophobic interaction, but before that there has been some light irony in Mr John Knightley's teasing of his father-in-law, a kind of reflex release of the tension caused by his fears about the weather. Knightley once again reveals that *he* is the person whose *real* sense of responsibility and moral concern are shown by his taking the trouble to investigate the *real* state of the conditions outside. The irony of course embraces Emma in her new and unwanted situation. She is shocked by Mr Elton's proposal, but it is her pride and judgement that are being called into question. For the first time she can see the impropriety of her conduct, for Mr Elton's passion is certainly based on what he considers to be her encouragement. The mutual anger generated is convincingly shown – Elton is revealed for what he is, a shallow opportunist – and there is a wonderful pathos at the end of the chapter with Emma appreciating, after this crisis, the kind attentions of her family.

a perverse turn i.e. an unwelcome statement or attitude.
tête-à-tête Close, intimate conversation.
making violent love to her i.e. in the sense that he is telling her how much he loves her – no physical love-making is implied.
inebriety Drunkenness. But of course Mr Elton was sober.
supplication i.e. being humbly entreated or begged.

Revision questions on Chapters 11–15

1 Give an account of the part played by Mr John Knightley in these chapters.

2 Indicate the ways in which Jane Austen arouses our interest in Frank Churchill.

3 Show how Jane Austen indicates in these chapters that Emma is deluding herself. Quote in support of your statements.

4 Write an account of any dramatic scene in these chapters.

5 Write an essay on the variety of Jane Austen's humour in these five chapters.

Chapter 16

Emma goes back in her mind over the past events with Harriet, Mr Elton and herself. She acknowledges Mr John Knightley's insight about Mr Elton's intentions, remembers the elder Mr Knightley's assertion that Mr Elton would never marry indiscreetly, and is also forced to recognize her own errors. She despises his proposal to her, seeing the mercenary motives behind it, but she admits that her behaviour towards him has been wrong and comes for the first time to a realization that her attempts at matchmaking have been unwise. The next day is Christmas Day; Mr Knightley visits them, but the thought everpresent in Emma's mind is the problem of Harriet.

Commentary

The exclamations of the first paragraph indicate the intensity of Emma's reactions. She is forced, as we have seen from the summary above, to re-evaluate past events in her mind, and this marks an important stage in the education of her feelings. Emma's sense of her own status – her inherent snobbery in thinking that she is above Elton in position, breeding and substance – is complemented by Elton's snobbery in considering himself Harriet's superior. But Emma is compelled to self-honesty and self-awareness, acknowledging that she has been foolish in trying to bring Harriet and Elton together. Yet her rooted obstinacy tells her that she was right in counselling Harriet to reject Robert Martin. All Emma's reactions have the mark of being psychologically true to life, even her feeling that Christmas Day comes as a relief after her experience with Mr Elton.

jumble i.e. a muddle, with no logic to it.
aggrandize i.e. get more position and property.
complaisant Pleasantly satisfied, encouraging.
analogy The usual meaning is 'agreement' or 'similarity', but the word 'harmony' best fits here.
éclat i.e. display, noise.

Chapter 17

Mr and Mrs John Knightley leave, while Mr Elton also departs, in his case to Bath for a few weeks. Emma goes to Mrs Goddard's to break the news to Harriet. The latter takes it well – 'her grief was so truly artless' – and Emma brings her to Hartfield, intent on comforting her. Harriet, however, is still romantically in love with (an idealized) Mr Elton, as are all the teachers and older girls at Mrs Goddard's school. Emma now has to live with what she has done.

Commentary

We note Mr Elton's rudeness in excluding Emma from his note to Mr Woodhouse, a mark of his ill-breeding. By contrast, we admire Emma's moral courage in going straight to Harriet. Emma also feels shame for what she has done, an indication of her sensitivity. Harriet's reactions are somewhat cloying but pathetic, the irony being that she looks up to her *image* of Mr Elton, which is so distinct from the vulgar and selfish opportunist Elton is in reality. Emma reveals that she has a conscience which has been stirred on Harriet's behalf. She also has a fore-casting imagination of how Mr Elton will behave on his return. Emma is sensitive and the effect of her recent experiences is to make her vulnerable and a little more flexible than she was.

intelligence News.

Chapter 18

To the great disappointment of the Westons and Emma, Frank Churchill does not come to Highbury. Emma talks of this to Knightley, who believes that Frank Churchill could come if he wished to and that he can leave the Churchills 'whenever he thinks it worth his while'. Knightley stresses that it is Frank's duty to see his father, and suggests that he would merit respect if he announced his intention of doing so. Emma opposes this on account of Frank Churchill's dependent position in relation to the Churchills. Knightley counters this with the assertion that Frank is idle and weak. Emma thinks that Knightley is deliberately intent on thinking ill of the young man. Emma paints her own picture of what the young man is like, while

Knightley continues angry at the prospect of this 'puppy'. Emma is somewhat put out by his preconceived dislike.

Commentary

Though Emma is naturally interested in the non-arrival of Frank Churchill, we note that she is trying desperately to be herself, making an effort of will that we have to admire. The dialogue between Emma and Knightley is revealing of each. It shows the preconceptions and prejudices of both, Knightley in particular unconsciously displaying his feeling for Emma – and perhaps a little jealousy – the feeling that anticipates his later declaration of love for her. The dialogue also shows Knightley's insight into motive and his basically right moral judgement concerning the need for a sense of duty. In fact he has an uncanny capacity for defining what turn out to be Frank Churchill's weaknesses later. At the same time we detect a certain irrational tone in his statements, and this again indicates his deep feeling for Emma and perhaps a wish to protect her from error in relation to Frank.

luxurious i.e. self-indulgent.
A little while ago he was at Weymouth . . . An unobtrusive plot hint – we are to learn he was present while Jane Fairfax was there, so that the attentive reader has a clue to their possible romance.
finessing Bringing about by artfulness.
shifts i.e. changes, manoeuvres.
'aimable' Charming (French).
nice Particular, discriminating.
conversible i.e. capable of holding a conversation.

Chapter 19

Emma and Harriet call on Mrs and Miss Bates. The latter quickly gets to the subject of Jane Fairfax's letter and tells Emma, after many diversions of her own making, that Jane is to come to stay with them for three months. There is some account of Jane and her relationship with Colonel and Mrs Campbell and their daughter Mrs Dixon, who is married to the man who had saved Jane's life while they were on holiday. Jane, we learn, has not been well for some time.

Commentary

The ramblings of Miss Bates and the speculation about Jane Fairfax – compare this with the speculation about Frank Churchill – provide the narrative interest, the entertainment and humour of the chapter. Miss Bates is over talkative, her remarks largely irrelevant; she is anxiously polite, a great gossip and conveyor of information. Her pride in Jane and her continual chatter about her have the effect of provoking Emma, who wickedly affects to believe that Jane may be in love with the Mr Dixon who saved her life. This shows that Emma has both imagination and spirit, a kind of refreshing devilry about her. Emma is also secretly delighted that she has escaped hearing the recital of Jane's letter.

beaufet A sideboard or cupboard, often containing food (hence 'buffet').

putting forward i.e. putting herself out to speak in order to save Harriet the trouble.

huswife A pocket-case containing sewing materials – pronounced 'huzzif'.

crosses half . . . chequer-work i.e. continuing to write in the margin, but at right-angles to the rest of the letter, thus using all available space.

Holyhead Anglesey, North Wales, the port of departure for Ireland.

Chapter 20

The story of Jane Fairfax occupies this chapter. The child of Mrs Bates's youngest daughter, with both parents dead, she has been brought up by Colonel Campbell and his wife with their daughter. They cannot bear to part with her. The daughter marries Mr Dixon, and Jane determines to provide for herself when she reaches the age of twenty-one. She is, however, run down in health, and decides to spend her last months before taking a situation with her grandmother and aunt. Emma has met her in the past but has never liked her. She determines to try to like Jane when she visits this time, but she finds her cold, elegant, and rather more talented than herself. Emma discovers that Frank Churchill was at Weymouth at the same time as Jane, but from Jane herself she can discover nothing about him.

Commentary

This chapter affords a striking example of the *economy* of Jane Austen's style in its use of retrospect to fill in the details of Jane Fairfax's life. We note also the parallels between Jane and Frank Churchill, brought up away from their main families and yet ironically destined to come together. Colonel Campbell's generosity is another moral index to right behaviour and responsibility. Equally right is the family's lack of jealousy over Jane's superior beauty. There is a considered stress on Jane's uncertain health. The usual delightful irony plays over her stay, the 'freshness of a two years' absence' making up for the 'perfect novelty' which Frank Churchill had been expected to supply. An interesting contrast is drawn with Emma – Jane is distant, reserved, elegant, accomplished, while Emma feels some guilt at not really being able to like her. Her imagination continues to work on a possible attachment between Jane and Mr Dixon. But she finds the Bateses tedious and Jane's reticence annoying. She provides no fuel to light Emma's capacity for speculation and gossip, and for this 'Emma could not forgive her'.

fondling The special favourite.
promote i.e. make the move to part with her (Jane).
noviciate i.e. entering into a religious order. Note the image, which is expanded in such terms as 'sacrifice', 'penance and mortification', ironic comments on the lot of the governess.
work-bags These presumably held wool, sewing etc.

Revision questions on Chapters 16–20

1 Describe Emma's reactions on the day after her encounter with Mr Elton.

2 Write an account of Harriet's reception of the news about Mr Elton.

3 How far do you think Mr Knightley's reactions to Frank Churchill's non-arrival are conditioned by his own interest in Emma? You should refer to the text in your answer.

4 In what ways do you find Miss Bates a comic character? Refer closely to Chapter 19 in your answer.

5 Compare and contrast Emma and Jane Fairfax as they are revealed in Chapter 20.

Chapter 21

Mr Knightley calls next day on business with Mr Woodhouse, and expresses his pleasure in the previous evening and his liking for Jane Fairfax. Emma conveys her compassion for her and, just as Knightley is about to tell Emma some news, Miss Bates and Jane Fairfax arrive with the announcement that Mr Elton is to be married to a Miss Hawkins. Miss Bates, as might be expected, is full of this news, delighting in the prospect of a new neighbour. Her flood of speculation is only occasionally interrupted. When she and Jane leave they are succeeded by another visitor – Harriet – who also brings news, this time of her frustrating meeting with Robert Martin and his sister. There was, in the words of Jane Austen, 'an interesting mixture of wounded affection and genuine delicacy in their behaviour' (p.148). Emma then breaks the news to Harriet of Mr Elton's approaching marriage.

Commentary

This chapter is full of comedy and narrative speed, the two items of news – Mr Elton's coming marriage and Harriet's meeting with Robert Martin and his sister – providing a kind of structural parallel. Contrast is of the essence here, with Mr Woodhouse as usual thinking of his diet (and of helping the Bateses with a gift of pork) and Miss Bates as garrulous as ever. There is a balance too between Knightley's rational appraisal of the previous evening and Emma's determination to be generous about Jane to him. Jane's silence and reticence of course contrast with her aunt's voluble recital. Narrative tension is maintained throughout, and there is something pathetic in Miss Bates's need for the excitement of the news. Ironically, Harriet's account of her meeting has a degree of pathos too, though we feel that Emma must be somewhat disconcerted by the fact that Harriet is obviously still very interested in Robert Martin. Emma is forced once more to rethink her position with regard to the Martins, and experiences relief that the news of Mr Elton's coming marriage is somewhat cushioned by Harriet's meeting with them.

spencer Close-fitting jacket.
salting-pan i.e. in which the pork would be cured.
'our lot is cast in a goodly heritage' A misquotation from, but retaining the spirit of, Psalm 16.

conduce Act together.
fancy Imagination.

Chapter 22

Much speculation in the village about Miss Hawkins's wealth and beauty when Mr Elton returns for a brief visit before he sets off for Bath to be married. Emma meets him, continues to dislike his airs, but feels that once he is married things will be better. Emma learns that Mr Elton's bride-to-be is the younger of two daughters of a Bristol merchant, and that her only claim to real status is her sister's marriage to a gentleman who keeps two carriages. Harriet is much put out by the reappearance of Mr Elton, and of course she has to endure much talk about him. But Elizabeth Martin leaves a note for Harriet at Mrs Goddard's, and Emma persuades Harriet to return the visit though she has doubts about whether she is doing the right thing.

Commentary

The opening of the chapter is informed by a delightful irony, which plays over the nature of the gossip about the future Mrs Elton. Mr Elton's shallowness and complacency as the successful suitor of an heiress are stressed, together with his self-conceit and insensitivity. Emma's reactions are predictably critical, for she feels a mixture of guilt and humiliation and is anxious to put her relationship with this rather worthless man on a new and formal footing once he is married. It is typical of Emma's own snobbery that she should judge Miss Hawkins before she has seen her in order to comfort herself – 'She brought no name, no blood, no alliance.' Emma remains concerned for Harriet, and Harriet herself almost indulges her lost love, the repetitive use of the word 'just' conveying her anguish. Thus Emma's dilemma is upon her; she sees the Martins, whom she once looked down upon – and still does, though with qualifications – as perhaps Harriet's solace for the loss of Mr Elton. The education of Emma's feelings and judgement continues.

always be called ten Note the irony, which implies distortion whenever there is gossip about money.
rencontre Meeting (French).
a great way i.e. comfortably off.

Chapter 23

Emma takes Harriet to meet the Martins. She picks her up after a short stay, before Harriet has had time to break the ice. Harriet broods on their reactions and her previous visit to them. After finding the Westons out, Emma and Harriet meet them on the road. They are greeted with the news that Frank Churchill will arrive the next day to stay for a fortnight. Emma is naturally restored to animation by this. Frank arrives a day early and is taken to Hartfield. Emma finds him charming and thinks that she will like him. He knows what to say to please her, refers to his 'home' as being Randalls, and greatly pleases Emma by speaking so well of Mrs Weston. She contemplates the possibility that he thinks of what other people might expect from a meeting between Frank Churchill and Emma Woodhouse. Mr Weston is obviously proud of his son. He leaves to do business at the Crown Inn, and Frank goes with him in order to visit Jane Fairfax, whom he has met at Weymouth.

Commentary

Harriet's capacity for misery is emphasized by her visit to the Martins, though there is some excuse for it, since she is allowed fourteen minutes of conversation with them and constantly recurs to her stay of six weeks with them earlier. Emma shows that she is irritated by all this and the impact of Mr Elton's news, but again Jane Austen's narrative art is in evidence when the meeting with the Westons brings the news of Frank's impending stay. Thereafter there is no flagging of interest. Note Emma's imaginative participation in what Mrs Weston is feeling at the time that Frank is due to arrive, and the unexpected twist of his early arrival. Emma is quick to respond, though one feels that even *she* finds some of his remarks rather glib. Emma is sensitive as to what may be construed about her and Frank, but is clear-sighted enough to free Mr Weston from any suspicion on this account. The visit by Frank to see Jane is a further quiet indication of their relationship: better still is the unconscious irony when all express the wish that he will go, since Jane and Miss Bates are in somewhat reduced circumstances and will appreciate the good breeding and good manners of the call.

espalier Lattice-work fences on which fruit trees are trained.
doubtingly i.e. with reserve, uncertainly.
unexceptionable There was nothing to find fault with (in them).
proportionably i.e. had progressed as a result.

Chapter 24

Frank Churchill and Mrs Weston pay a call on Emma the following morning. They walk round Hartfield, with Frank praising everything that he sees. When they stop at the Crown Inn, Frank remarks on the suitability of the ballroom – now in abeyance as a whist club – and suggests that a ball should be held every fortnight. Emma objects that there are insufficient people of real rank in the district, but Frank overrides this, so much so that she considers that he has a lack of fitting pride. They pass the Bateses, and Frank tells of his visit the previous day. In response to Emma's question, he says that he thought Jane Fairfax looked 'very ill'. As Emma carries on with her questions, he hurriedly breaks off and they enter Ford's shop, where he buys a pair of gloves.

Emma persists in asking Frank about his acquaintance with Jane at Weymouth and though he prevaricates, he admits that he was much in her society and says that he likes the Campbells. After he and Emma have both praised Jane's piano playing, he also reveals that Mr Dixon preferred Jane's playing to that of his fiancée Miss Campbell. This is fuel for Emma's idea of an attachment between Jane and Mr Dixon, but Frank says that Miss Campbell did not resent Jane's superior accomplishment. Emma acknowledges that because of Jane's reserve she has been unable to get friendly with her. Frank observes that 'One cannot love a reserved person' (p.166). Emma finds herself warming towards him, particularly when he remarks that Mr Elton's house was one to be shared with the woman one loves. This leads Emma to think that Frank himself intends to marry soon.

Commentary

Emma is satisfied that Frank is taking due account of Mrs Weston, but the reader notes what Emma in part feels, though she will not admit it – that Frank is somewhat indiscriminate in his praise of everything. Frank is an enthusiast for dancing, as we see from the visit to the Crown Inn, and a brilliant stylistic effect captures the flow of his language almost verbatim as the idea of a regular ball takes hold of him. Emma's own snobbery and consciousness of status is shown when she considers him to be without pride. Frank's admission that he spent three-quarters of an hour with the Bateses is a plot hint as to his interest in Jane, though he is hypocrite enough to cover any suggestion of this by describing her as having 'A most deplorable want of complexion' (p.163).

Frank's move into Ford's is an attempt to put an end to the discussion on Jane and Weymouth, but Emma is obstinate, persistent, determined. Note that Emma's wish that Jane may be in love with Mr Dixon underlines the fact that she is as wrongheaded as ever. There is a revealing moment when Frank acknowledges that he knows Jane is destined to be a governess. The irony continues when Emma observes that Jane's feelings 'are known to no human being, I guess', since she is talking to the one human being to whom they are known. Emma's honesty about her own feelings for Jane is commendable, but we notice that she is romancing in her own mind about Frank.

construction i.e. interpretation.
post-horses Horses kept at the inns along the roads ready to carry passengers and mail by coach to the next stage. They appear to have been used for local journeys at Highbury.
sashed i.e. having sash-cords.
environs Neighbourhood.
half a guinea 52½p, but worth very much more in Jane Austen's time.
'Men's Beavers' . . . 'York Tan' Goods for sale, probably hats and gloves.
amor patriae Love of one's country (Latin).
cried up Praised.

Chapter 25

Emma's good opinion of Frank Churchill is undermined the next day when she hears that he has suddenly gone off to London for a haircut. Mrs Weston obviously thinks highly of her stepson, and Mr Weston further mollifies Emma by telling her how much Frank admires her. Although all around think lightly of Frank's whim, Knightley considers him to be a 'trifling, silly fellow'. Emma is asked to dine by Mr and Mrs Cole. She looks down on them somewhat because their money has been made in trade, but her friends will be there and she is pleased when Mr and Mrs Weston urge her to accept. Mr Woodhouse declines the invitation and it is arranged that Mrs Goddard will sit with him for the evening. He urges Emma to come away from the Coles before she is too tired; she refuses to leave early since it might offend the Coles, and Mr Woodhouse fusses about her and about himself.

Commentary

Frank's sudden action calls for moral comment, at least to herself, from Emma, but she continues to romanticize, liking to think that despite her own indifference – also affected – Frank is, if not in love with her, at least near it. The author's irony suggests that Mr Weston's pride in this son is defensible, and that the parishes of Donwell and Highbury can excuse 'one who smiled so often and bowed so well'. Emma even shows restraint when Knightley diminishes Frank by his comments, and there is also her vacillation over the Coles' invitation when she realizes that Frank and Knightley have been invited too. She is pleased to put down her own snobbery, thus revealing a chink in her obstinacy which is to grow wider with experience. Mr Woodhouse's concern for her – and for himself – is typically within character, and provides some amusing moments in which his concern and uncertainties are delicately probed through the dialogue.

chaise Light open carriage for two.
coxcomb Foolish, vain person.
only moderately genteel Notice how this phrase perfectly captures Emma's snobbery and condescension.
folding screen One placed behind chairs to protect the sitters from draughts.
piquet A card game for two played with a pack of thirty-two cards.

Revision questions on Chapters 21–25

1 Write a clear account of the two main dramatic events in Chapter 21.

2 What do you learn of Emma's character from these chapters? Refer closely to the text in your answer.

3 What is your impression of Frank Churchill? Again, refer closely to the text to support your views.

4 In what ways does Jane Austen create narrative tension in Chapter 24?

Chapter 26

Frank Churchill returns, and Emma looks forward to seeing him at the Coles', thinking how she will discourage his attentions. Mrs Bates as well as Mrs Goddard sit with Mr Woodhouse for the evening. Emma arrives just after Mr Knightley, is graciously received by the Coles, and Frank Churchill sits next to her at dinner. Mrs Cole talks of the piano that Jane Fairfax has just received as an unexpected gift. There is general conversation, Colonel Campbell being considered the likely donor, but Emma considers that the gift has come from Mr Dixon, and confides to Frank that she believes that Mr Dixon is in love with Jane. Frank himself says that he observed Mr Dixon save Jane's life, and after dinner the party is joined by Jane, Harriet and Miss Bates. After more discussion of the piano, Frank sits by Emma and tells her about Enscombe. When he goes to speak to Jane, Mrs Weston joins Emma and tells her that Knightley had arranged for Jane and Miss Bates to be brought in his carriage. His carriage is also to take them home, and Mrs Weston confides to Emma that she believes Knightley is in love with Jane and has sent her the piano. Emma cannot agree with this. After taking tea Emma plays the piano and sings. Frank unexpectedly joins in, and Jane then plays and sings with Frank. Following this the room is cleared for dancing. Mrs Weston plays a waltz, and Emma leads off with Frank. It is late now, and after two dances the party ends and the guests leave.

Commentary

Emma reads into Frank's behaviour just what she wants to, and there is a considered irony about her decision to treat him rather coolly. Of course she doesn't, though an indication of her later awakening feelings for Knightley is shown by her pleasure in the fact that he has come to the Coles' party in his carriage 'like a gentleman'. There is a delightful and brief interplay of humour between Emma and Knightley. Emma is delighted to be singled out by Frank (so much for her intended reserve!). Once again Jane Austen produces the unexpected – narrative tension is raised by the mysterious gift of the Broadwood piano to Jane Fairfax. Mrs Cole proves to be almost as garrulous as Miss Bates. A kind of dramatic irony plays over the dialogue between Emma and Frank Churchill in the light of the plot development, since we later discover that it is Frank who has sent the piano. Here he is deliberately encouraging Emma in her erroneous conclusion that it comes from Mr Dixon. Yet we note too the naturalness of this dialogue. Emma exults in Harriet's prettiness as she enters, but is not so pleased when Harriet compares Frank Churchill's looks to Mr Elton's! Although Emma feels she is being singled out by Frank Churchill, his approach to Jane Fairfax again underlines the movement of the plot – he goes to see her apparently to tell her that he doesn't like her hair-style, a singularly unconvincing move. Knightley's kindness in providing the carriage is liable to misinterpretation, though Emma rightly considers it 'good-natured, useful, considerate'. Mrs Weston takes on Emma's role as match-maker in her pairing of Jane and Knightley. For a moment Emma reveals her feelings – 'Mr Knightley must not marry!' – and her jealousy of the fact that Jane would be mistress of the Abbey. The whole of this dialogue gives a direct insight into Emma's heart, her unknown and unvoiced love for Knightley being quite apparent to the reader. She is so upset that she mimics Miss Bates in a somewhat bitter anticipation of that lady's likely reaction to a marriage between her niece and Knightley. Emma's conversation with Knightley convinces her that he did not send the piano, but his manifestation of concern for Jane's voice and health – as well as his attacking Frank Churchill for getting her to sing too much – does not please Emma. She is relieved, however, that he doesn't dance with Jane.

coxcomb See note p.48.
spinnet (Usually spelt 'spinet'.) Keyed musical instrument like the harpsichord with one string to each note.
entrapped i.e. gathered, understood.
en passant In passing (French).
naiveté Lack of sophistication (French).
outrée Eccentric, unsuitable (French).
cut out i.e. excluded from the inheritance of.
put to i.e. turn out.

Chapter 27

Emma ponders on her own inferiority to Jane Fairfax in her playing and singing, and practises for some time until interrupted by Harriet. The latter praises her playing, and tells her that Mr Martin has dined with the Coxes recently. Emma and Harriet go shopping at Ford's, and while Harriet is considering a purchase, Emma stands at the door and sees Frank Churchill and Mrs Weston in the street. After a brief chat they leave her to visit the Bateses, to hear Jane's piano. Harriet makes her purchase after a great deal of indecision; she and Emma are just leaving when they are met by Miss Bates and Mrs Weston, who entreat them to go and listen to the piano. Miss Bates talks at great length and without any discrimination on a variety of subjects, the two most important of which are Frank Churchill's repairing of her mother's spectacles and Knightley's gift of apples.

Commentary

A delightful irony encompasses Emma's impetuous but unsustained practising and Harriet's undiscriminating praise of it. We note that Harriet is still greatly drawn to Robert Martin and that Emma senses the danger, even going to Ford's with Harriet to protect her from a stray meeting in the street. We also note that Frank Churchill manipulates his mother-in-law about the visit to the Bateses, and cunningly gets Emma's approval for it too. Obviously he is trying to make his attentions to Jane Fairfax appear natural and uncontrived. Harriet's shallow nature and her vacillation are seen in her delay over her purchase, while Miss Bates is seen at her best – and worst – as she ranges over all subjects within her verbal reach, including Jane's health. This should be studied carefully, as Miss Bates represents the high point of Jane Austen's comic art, but with the indication that all the talk covers the pathos of uncertainty.

execution i.e. skill.
letter-boy A boy sent out to deliver the letters in an outlying area.
the medley A superb piece of irony to indicate the ramblings of Miss Bates's thought.
keeping An apple that would last well into the winter without going bad.

Chapter 28

In the Bates's sitting-room Frank Churchill is mending the spectacles, Jane looking at her piano, and Emma is quickly welcomed. Jane plays and, after she has finished, they all admire the piano. Frank teases Jane about the gift, and asks her to play a waltz. She does so, and Frank continues to tease her by reminding her that the same waltz was played at Weymouth, whereupon she colours deeply. Emma wishes that he would stop embarrassing Jane, but he continues with his flippancy. Miss Bates sees Mr Knightley outside the window on horseback, engages him in conversation, and Knightley replies by asking after Jane Fairfax. Invited in by Miss Bates, he appears about to come, but when he learns that she already has company – and more particularly Frank Churchill – he makes his excuses and proceeds on his way to Kingston. Before he does so Miss Bates manages to convey, among other things, her loquacious thanks for the gift of apples.

Commentary

Emma feels some pity for Jane over the piano and even more during Frank Churchill's teasing of her. Frank Churchill enjoys the sound of his own voice and we, and Emma, detect a degree of insensitivity in his constant innuendo with Jane. All the hints of their concealed relationship are uttered by Frank, though only Jane is aware of them, and she is intent on concealment while Frank enjoys this flirting with danger. Of course he is covering his own tracks by the constant references to Colonel Campbell. Nevertheless his implications are perhaps self-congratulatory too, as when he says 'True affection only could have prompted it' (p.196). There is a semi-comic interaction with Mr Knightley, since the listeners in the room can hear everything that is said. There is enough too to keep Emma guessing in Knightley's obvious concern for Jane Fairfax's health and his equally strong wish not to be in Frank Churchill's company.

deedily Actively.
Cramer Johann Baptist (1771–1858), English musician of German extraction, founder of the London music publishing house of Cramer and Co.

Robin Adair An 18th-century lyric by Lady Caroline Keppel.
described Saw.
Kingston Then a market town on the Thames some ten miles south-
west of London.

Chapter 29

Frank Churchill proposes a dance at Randalls. Emma, Frank
and Mr Woodhouse discuss the question of the numbers to be
invited. This takes a lengthy turn, but next morning Frank
himself appears at Hartfield with the solution: to avoid over-
crowding, Mr Weston has suggested that the ball be held at the
Crown Inn. Mr Woodhouse fears the damp of an inn room, but
is somewhat reassured when he is told that Mrs Weston will be in
charge and that she will see to it that the place is aired. Emma
and Frank meet Mrs Weston at the Crown and investigate the
practical difficulties. Despite Mrs Weston's objections it is ultimately settled, with her agreement, that the dance will be held at
the Crown; Frank claims Emma for the first two dances.

Commentary

We note Frank's enthusiasm, and Emma's delight at the prospect of again being seen with him in public, balanced by Mr
Woodhouse's caution and apprehensions – he has a neurotic
fear of draughts. Frank further shows his obstinacy and determination in pursuing the matter, even Emma noticing that 'the
nature of his gallantry was a little self-willed' (p.201). There is
much humour in Mr Woodhouse's own determined opposition
to the plan of having the dance at the Crown, but of course his
faith in Mrs Weston's capability leads him to sympathetic consideration in the end. There is also some ironic humour in the
serious examination of the practicalities, almost as if such ser-
iousness over something superficial is misplaced. Frank again
manages to get himself into Jane's company – another plot hint
here – but Mr Weston obviously feels that Frank's interest is in
Emma.

Chapter 30

Frank's wish to stay is apparently not opposed from Enscombe,
but Mr Knightley expresses indifference to the whole scheme,

though he agrees to be there. Emma is made rather angry by his attitude. Jane Fairfax is looking forward to the ball, and Emma therefore is free to take the view that Mrs Weston is wrong in thinking that Mr Knightley is in love with Jane. Suddenly comes the news that Frank has to leave for Enscombe, since his aunt is ill. The ball is postponed, Frank visits Hartfield to say farewell to Emma, and she is convinced that he is on the edge of proposing to her when they are interrupted by Mr Weston. After he has gone Emma realizes how much she will miss him, and persuades herself that she is a little in love with him.

Commentary

This short chapter contains an insight into the reactions of Mr Knightley and Emma, the latter relieved that he is not apparently interested in Jane Fairfax, and he more concerned with business and the practical use of time rather than wasting it on frippery. At the same time it perhaps reveals his jealousy of Emma's interest in Frank Churchill. The latter's having to go comes as a surprise, though such is Jane Austen's narrative control that it has always been a possibility. All his remarks to Emma contain that ambiguity which makes for tension – Emma believes that his regret is on account of her, but later events will of course reveal that it was inspired by his love for Jane Fairfax. There is a telling focus on Emma's misreading of the situation. Knightley is in fact kind but cheerful at what has occurred, but Emma still cannot penetrate the composure of Jane Fairfax.

Revision questions on Chapters 26–30

1 Give a detailed account of the dinner party at the Coles, clearly indicating the part played in it by Frank Churchill.

2 What clues are to be found in these chapters which indicate Frank Churchill's interest in Jane Fairfax?

3 Write an essay on any two or three dramatic incidents in these chapters.

4 In what ways do you consider that Emma is still deluding herself?

Chapter 31

Emma ponders on her love for Frank Churchill, but decides that it is not very deep, so continues cheerful. She engages in imaginary proposals from him, but always ends by refusing them! She remains assured, however, that Frank is in love with her, though she does allow that his feelings may not be constant. Mrs Weston receives a letter from Frank in which he compares Highbury and Enscombe, says some complimentary things about Emma, but is unable to fix a time for coming to Randalls again because of Mrs Churchill's illness. Emma even speculates on Harriet as being a possible future partner for Frank. Village speculation now centres upon 'Mr Elton and his bride', with Harriet distressed by the strength of her feelings for Elton. Emma comforts her, and is greatly moved by Harriet's tenderness and affection.

Commentary

A wonderful insight into Emma's feelings; her sense of fun; her acknowledgement that she is not deeply in love; her imaginative capacity; her fantasies; her determination. Yet when temptation comes to match-make again on Harriet's behalf, she almost gives in to it despite the dreadful warning of her previous venture. But she is deeply honest about herself, capable of misjudgement with regard to Frank and, ironically, says to herself 'happy the man who changes Emma for Harriet!' They are significant words, and she is to see the significance poignantly later when Knightley appears to be showing interest in her poor little friend.

Chapter 32

Emma and Harriet visit the newly-married Eltons. After they have left, Harriet expresses her feeling that Elton is 'just as superior as ever'. But when the Eltons return the visit by coming to Hartfield, Emma considers Mrs Elton to be a vain, ill-mannered, ignorant woman. She monopolizes the conversation, speaking of her brother-in-law's two carriages and his house, and she condescends to Mr Woodhouse. She suggests that he should try Bath for his health, and includes Emma in her patronage by saying that she could introduce her to the best society there. Her own resources are such that she won't mind the lack of society of Highbury after the luxury of Maple Grove. She even proposes to Emma that they form a music club, but compounds her ill-breeding by saying that she has visited Randalls and was surprised to find Mrs Weston so ladylike, while her meeting with her 'caro sposo's' friend Knightley confirms the latter to be a 'gentleman-like man'. Emma's word after she has gone is 'Insufferable' and it best fits this loquacious snob. Mr Woodhouse has only found her quickness of speech difficult to follow, and is somewhat depressed to think that his health will prevent him from visiting the Vicarage before summer.

Commentary

The uneasiness of the visit to the Eltons is well conveyed, with a superbly focused wit on Elton's being, at the same time, in the same room 'with the woman he had just married, the woman he had wanted to marry, and the woman whom he had been expected to marry' (p.217). After Harriet's pathetic reaction and her over valuation of Mr Elton, Mrs Elton is displayed in all her vulgar vainglory, for she is self-important, smug, foolish, ignorant, snobbish. She talks almost as much as Miss Bates, and always with the idea of self-advancement, in her own excellence, or through her exalted connections. Maple Grove comes before her caro sposo, she is ill-informed, inaccurate, boastful, materialistic, totally insincere, affecting to be what she is not. Her condescension infuriates Emma – 'The dignity of Miss Woodhouse, of Hartfield, was sunk indeed!' (p.220). She sees into and through Mrs Elton, realizing that the proposal for a music club is so that Mrs Elton can in effect neglect her music. Emma's words sum her up perfectly. 'A little upstart, vulgar being' (p.223). Typically, Mr Woodhouse does not see through her at all. Emma broods long on Mrs Elton's imperfections. Emma is certainly being educated by experience.

Surry is the garden of England Typical of Mrs Elton's inaccuracy –
  Kent is usually considered to be the garden of England.
barouche-landau A four-wheeled carriage with an adjustable hood, so
  arranged that two couples can be seated facing one another.
in so . . . a train So well organized.
caro sposo Dear husband (Italian).
nice Particular, finicky.

vanity-baits A particularly bitter expression for Emma, who is being made to feel by Mrs Elton that she, as a married woman, must take precedence everywhere.

Chapter 33

Emma continues to dislike the Eltons, a dislike increased by their unpleasant attitude towards Harriet. Mrs Elton is intent upon patronizing Jane Fairfax, and loses no opportunity to boast of her brother-in-law's carriages. Emma tries to put her off taking up Jane, and Mrs Elton's attitude towards Emma cools. Emma is surprised and amused by the fact that Jane Fairfax accepts the friendship of the Eltons apparently uncritically. She mentions this to Mrs Weston, who, however, feels that any change for Jane must be counted pleasure after the constant companionship of Miss Bates. Knightley would like Emma herself to pay more attention to Jane. He praises Jane, and Emma betrays her opinion that he may be in love with her. But this he denies. He admits her charm, but considers her too reserved to make a good wife.

Commentary

This marks the extension of Mrs Elton's patronage to Jane, her ill-breeding and that of her husband being shown in their attitude towards Harriet. There are some unconsciously witty statements by Mrs Elton herself — 'I am a great advocate for timidity' (p.226) — and Emma's moderate sarcasms fail to put her down. There is a mystery about Jane's refusal to join the Campbells in Ireland. Knightley shows his sound common sense in his appraisal of the relationship between Mrs Elton and Jane, but is somewhat put out by Emma's probing of his own relationship with Jane. Even here he is modest, saying that Jane would not accept him if he did propose, which he has no intention of doing. There is a delightful interaction of foot-pressing between Emma and Mrs Weston while this is going on. Thus heartened Emma ranges wittily over Mrs Elton's faults, but Mrs Weston remains unconvinced, feeling that Knightley may end up by being in love with Jane.

conjugal unreserve i.e. the Eltons had talked unreservedly of Harriet's infatuation for Mr Elton.

knight-errantry Chivalrous intentions (here, heavily sarcastic).
'Full many a flower . . .' A slight misquotation from Gray's famous
 'Elegy Written in a Country Churchyard' (1751) – for 'fragrance' in
 the second line read 'sweetness'.

Chapter 34

The Eltons, much to Mrs Elton's delight, receive many invitations, and she arranges one 'very superior party' as a means of
returning them. Before that Emma manages to entertain them
at Hartfield; Harriet wishes to remain at home, so Emma invites
Jane Fairfax in her place. Mr John Knightley is also to come on
that very day, but Mr Weston is required to be in town on
business. Mr Woodhouse, concerned about the numbers at dinner, is now satisfied that there will be the proper number of
eight. John Knightley talks much to Jane, who reveals that she
pays a daily visit to the post office. She is obviously touched by
John Knightley's kindness to her. Mr Woodhouse, seconded by
Mrs Elton, expresses much concern that such visits mean that
Jane is out in the rain. Mrs Elton officiously tries to impose her
man's getting the letters for Jane, but the latter resolutely resists
the arrangement. There follows a discussion on the postal service and different hand-writing. Emma praises Frank
Churchill's but Knightley thinks that it is effeminate. Mrs Elton
leads the way into dinner, and Emma continues solicitous on
Jane's account.

Commentary

The invitations establish Mrs Elton in a position of condescension, since she has set ideas about the *right* way to do things,
which she intends to demonstrate at her own party. Emma is
resolved to do her duty and entertain the Eltons; she shows her
sensitivity on Harriet's account – in view of their attitude
towards her Harriet would hardly like to be in the Eltons' company – and Emma appeases her conscience by inviting Jane. The
post office visits are an important plot hint (Jane is hoping for a
letter from Frank Churchill) and Jane's blushing and resolve not
to be denied her daily visit give an indication of her need. John
Knightley typically reveals his kindness and, such is Jane's
tremulous state, she is easily moved by it. Mrs Elton blunders
into the situation with her usual loud insensitivity, but Jane has

wit enough to turn the discussion. The debate on hand-writing reveals Knightley's uncompromising attitude towards Frank, while the close of the chapter has a delightful irony, with Emma thinking that Jane's letter may have come from Ireland. She is still following out her mistaken idea that Jane is in love with Mr Dixon.

rout-cakes Party cakes.
post-office In 1710 an act of Queen Anne consolidated the posts into one establishment. In 1784 John Palmer introduced a system of fast mail-coaches with armed guards, which lessened the likelihood of robbery.
variety of hands i.e. differences in handwriting.
expedition and the expense of the Irish mails i.e. the speed, efficiency and cost of the Irish postal services. Emma is following out her suspicion indicated above. She is very wide of the mark.

Chapter 35

Mrs Elton slights Emma and pays attention only to Jane Fairfax after dinner, further imposing on her by saying that she will get her a situation. Jane resists, Mrs Elton is adamant, becoming more insistent and vociferous. After that Emma hears her say of Mr Woodhouse 'Here comes this dear old beau of mine', and she continues with her vulgar remarks, praising 'a simple style of dress', hers of course being the very reverse. Mr Weston has returned and joins the party, Mr John Knightley being amazed that after a day in town he should choose to leave his own fireside. He has brought a letter from Frank indicating that he will shortly be in town with the Churchills and will thus be able to spend much of his time at Randalls.

Commentary

Mrs Elton's insensitivity about Jane's situation, as well as her snobbery, are prominently in evidence at the beginning of this chapter, but there is also some biting moral comment on what Jane calls, rather dejectedly, the 'governess-trade'. She again pleads that nothing should be done for her, at least for two or three months, and this is perhaps a further hint of her involvement with Frank Churchill, or at least her hopes of an engagement to him being publicly acknowledged. The gross ill-manners and vulgarity of Mrs Elton are shown in her conceited reference to Mr Woodhouse. We note with some amusement the mixed reactions to the news that Frank Churchill will soon be among them again. Perhaps most amusing of all is Emma's thinking that her own agitation at the news is 'considerable'.

Wax-candles i.e. indicating expense (they were dearer than tallow-candles) which of course Mrs Elton would not like to see wasted on a mere schoolroom.
slave-trade Slavery was not officially abolished until 1833.
condition for i.e. make a point of insisting upon.
caro sposo See note p.56.
the black gentleman i.e. the Devil.
Put it up i.e. finish with it (the letter).

Revision questions on Chapters 31–35

1 Describe Emma's reactions after the departure of Frank Churchill.

2 Give an account of the character of Mrs Elton as it is revealed in these chapters.

3 In what ways do you feel sorry for Jane Fairfax? You should refer closely to the text in your answer.

4 Write a detailed account of any important conversation in any of these chapters, giving your reasons for finding it important.

5 Write an essay on Jane Austen's irony at the expense of either Emma or Mr Woodhouse.

Chapter 36

Mr Weston conveys to Mrs Elton the news of his son's coming visit, Mrs Churchill's illness and her desire for a change from the Yorkshire climate providing the reason for it. Mrs Elton is soon launched on the subject of her relations in Bath, Mr Weston countering with his doubts about the genuineness of Mrs Churchill's illness and remarking on her arrogance and lack of breeding. Mrs Elton is reminded of some newcomers near Maple Grove who have presumed to consider themselves on equal terms with her brother-in-law Mr Suckling. The conversation is somewhat stilted since she is intent on boasting about her relations while Mr Weston is anxious to praise his son. After this there is cards, conversation, then Mr John Knightley expresses the wish to Emma that she will not let her nephews be a burden to her during their stay.

Commentary

We note the humour in the exchanges between Mr Weston and Mrs Elton where the latter is almost put down by Mr Weston's believing her when she denies that her sister Selina is a fine lady! Her boastfulness and arrogance largely bounce off Mr Weston; in fact he is pleasantly egocentric over Frank, while she is unpleasantly egocentric over Mr Suckling and her materialistic connections. Mrs Elton is so self-centred that she virtually demands a compliment from Mr Weston, which that good-natured man obligingly pays. She indicates too that she is determined to patronize Frank Churchill, though she claims 'I am no flatterer' (p.247). Mr Weston's reply is not without irony, either his own or his author's, for his account of Mrs Churchill would aptly fit the lady to whom he is speaking; as he says, 'I assure you, she is an upstart' (p.247).

John Knightley again shows how considerate he is, and there is some delightful raillery at Emma's expense from Knightley himself as well as from his brother – the implication being, in a teasing way, that her social life has much expanded. Emma rises to the bait, but also asserts that her nephews come before everything, a natural insight into her own capacity for marriage and domesticity which – she says earlier – she has chosen to forgo.

nicety i.e. being particular.
Clifton A spa overlooking the Avon near Bristol.
Hymen's saffron robe Hymen was the God of marriage in classical mythology. Greek and Roman brides wore a saffron veil which wholly enveloped them.
Tea was carrying round Note the construction, typical of Jane Austen, meaning 'Tea was being carried round.'
physic i.e. give them medicine.

Chapter 37

Emma ponders on the coming return of Frank Churchill, feeling that he is bound to propose to her and wishing she could keep him from an outright declaration. When Frank arrives he appears less interested in Emma than hitherto. Mrs Churchill's health is not improved by London, and after ten days they decide to move to Richmond. Frank, who has been unable to visit Randalls again, writes of this change of plan. Mr Weston is delighted that his son will only be some nine miles away from them. Preparations for the postponed ball to be held at the Crown get under way again.

Commentary

Once more Emma is proved wrong in her calculations, for what she thinks Frank will immediately do he proceeds not to do. She puts it all down to her own indifference to him, and we note that although Emma's feelings are in the process of being educated she still continues remarkably blind and inaccurate in her speculations. Even Frank's restlessness she traces to herself, having no knowledge of why he is really in a flutter. Though she is set on rejection, she is aware that in Mr Weston's eyes a union between herself and Frank would be a happy consummation.

Richmond Now a large residential suburb of south-west London.
Manchester street In the parish of Marylebone, central London.

Chapter 38

At the request of Mr Weston, Emma arrives early with Harriet on the evening of the ball. He wants her advice on the arrangements and, together with other arrivals, they inspect and admire what has been done. When the Eltons appear it turns out they have forgotten to pick up Miss Bates and Jane Fairfax, but Frank Churchill goes back in their carriage to collect them. Miss Bates launches into a monologue, addressing the company in general while Mrs Elton, who believes that the ball is being given in her honour, takes it upon herself to assist Mrs Weston in welcoming the guests. She also opens the dancing with Mr Weston while Emma, who had hoped for this honour, follows in their wake with Frank. She notices Mr Knightley looking on, admires his bearing, and wishes he would join in the dancing. Harriet is without a partner, and Mr Elton deliberately slights her by refusing Mrs Weston's request that he should dance with her. Emma sees Mr and Mrs Elton exchange delighted looks at this cruel snub; then, to her great delight, she sees Mr Knightley ask Harriet to dance. Miss Bates later tells Frank and Jane that she has been back to put her mother to bed after keeping Mr Woodhouse company. After supper Emma makes a point of thanking Mr Knightley for his kindness to Harriet, admitting that she was mistaken in her early favourable impression of Mr Elton. Mr Knightley, generally a non-dancing man, then asks Emma to dance with him.

Commentary

Emma is of course complimented by being the first to survey the rooms at the Crown, though when she finds that others have also been similarly complimented, we notice that a light ironical tone plays over her vanity. Mrs Elton is able to approve of Frank, but her basic lack of consideration is shown in their having forgotten to pick up Miss Bates and Jane Fairfax, thus causing inconvenience. Miss Bates is not put out; her ready flow has all the unconscious humour of indiscriminate talk, hers ranging backwards and forwards from the present to the past with constant appeals to Jane for confirmation – confirmation for which, of course, she doesn't wait. Mrs Elton solicits a compliment from Frank, but addresses Jane familiarly, to the disgust of Frank who overhears her. The plan is for Mr Weston to take in Mrs Elton – this saves Frank from doing so – and a delightful authorial comment defines Emma's response to being placed second – 'It was almost enough to make her think of marrying' (p.257). But note that Emma always has an eye on Mr Knightley, a measure of her interest in him. She notes too that he watches her, a measure of his interest in her. She is now even more certain that Frank values her less than he has done. Emma's concern for Harriet is generously complemented by that of Mrs Weston; Mr Elton's response is both ill-mannered and ill-bred. By contrast Knightley's good manners, courtesy and complete understanding of Harriet's position prove him to be the gentleman we know he is. Miss Bates's second contribution is largely in miscellaneous commentary on Jane's doings. Emma and Knightley reach a deeper understanding and a shared condemnation of Mr Elton. Emma acknowledges that she was completely mistaken in him, and Knightley acknowledges that he has underrated Harriet.

These admissions reflect the integrity of both, an integrity that later leads to increased compatibility.

privy counsellors i.e. close advisers.
puppyism i.e. spoilt behaviour.
tippet A garment, usually of fur or wool, covering the neck and shoulders.
fricassee of sweetbread An entrée composed of the pancreas of a lamb or calf, stewed, then sliced and fried, and served with a sauce.

Chapter 39

Emma is delighted that Knightley shares her opinion of the Eltons and that he has been kind to Harriet. She is also rather inclined to congratulate herself that Frank does not appear to be too much in love with her. She is just returning to the house when Frank comes up the drive with a pale and frightened Harriet on his arm. When they enter the house Harriet faints in the hall. It turns out that Harriet and a friend had been out walking when they encountered some gipsies. The friend fled back to Highbury but Harriet, who had got cramp after the ball, could not climb the bank to escape. She gives them a shilling to let her go, but the gipsies surround her and ask for more. Frank finds her terrified, drives the gipsies away, and brings her to Hartfield. Emma thinks – match-making is second nature to her – that the incident may make Frank and Harriet fall in love with each other.

Commentary

Emma is in self-congratulatory mood, contemplating a happy summer, when the dramatic incident of the appearance of Frank and Harriet occurs. Again Jane Austen's narrative art embraces the unexpected, and notice the crisp economy which tells what has happened. The retrospect is just as swift in its filling in of detail as the first description, and Frank is cast in the role of hero rescuing heroine. Emma has her own ironic contemplation of this fact and what it will lead to. In fact the tone is mocking of the romantic type novel where such things *would* happen as part of plot furtherance. Emma now has another possibility of a romantic match within her sights, and this finely economic chapter closes with the gipsies disappearing as suddenly as they they came, perhaps indicating the ephemeral nature of the romance they have provided.

sweepgate See note p.35.
shilling In today's money 5p, but worth much more in Jane Austen's
  time.
imaginist One having a powerful imagination.
rencontre Encounter (French).

Chapter 40

Harriet calls on Emma a few days later with a small parcel. She obviously wants to confide in Emma, and produces a piece of court-plaster and a pencil. She has saved these as mementoes of Mr Elton, the plaster being left over after he had dressed his cut finger, while the pencil had actually belonged to him. This she tells Emma, adding that she cannot think how she was actually deceived in him; she does not wish them evil, but she doesn't care if she never sees the Eltons again. She throws the mementoes on the fire, and Emma begins to hope that this end will mark the beginning of her friendship with Frank Churchill. Harriet hints that she admires someone who is too superior to marry her. Emma jumps to the conclusion that she is referring to Frank and, while acknowledging his superiority, gives Harriet some food for hope.

Commentary

Not only is the novel about the education of Emma's feelings, it is about the education of Harriet's too. Harriet is somewhat impulsive in this exchange, but we appreciate her behaviour and her confiding in Emma – a less generous person might have blamed Emma for what actually happened. Although she is rational, Harriet has an embarrassing capacity for remembering what Emma has almost forgotten or would rather forget. Harriet asserts that she will never marry, and there follows one of those superbly ironic misunderstandings. Emma thinks that Harriet is speaking of Frank Churchill and encourages her; the reader may have other suspicions, for two people have 'saved' her recently. Ironically, these are Frank and Knightley, who asked her to dance.

Tunbridge-ware box A small box inlaid with sycamore and beechwood. Manufactured by a Tunbridge Wells company that began in 1685 to make toys, workboxes etc.

court plaister Sticking plaster made of silk, formerly used by ladies at court for face-patches.

spruce-beer A fermented drink made from the leaves and branches of the fir tree.

Revision questions on Chapters 36–40

1 What do you find humorous in the conversation between Mr Weston and Mrs Elton in Chapter 36?

2 Give an account of the behaviour of (a) The Eltons and (b) Mr Knightley at the ball.

3 Write a detailed examination of Jane Austen's style in Chapter 39.

4 In what ways do you find Emma still guilty of error? Refer closely to the text in your answer.

Chapter 41

It is now June, and it seems likely that Jane Fairfax will remain at Highbury for another two months. Mr Knightley believes that Frank Churchill is flirting with Jane Fairfax as well as Emma, and accordingly dislikes him the more. He has noted the meaningful looks exchanged between Frank and Jane at a dinner. He has also been quick enough to spot a slip of Frank's on their way to Hartfield, when he speaks of Mr Perry setting up his carriage, saying he knows this from a letter of Mrs Weston's. She says she knew nothing of it, but Miss Bates declares that both she and Jane knew of the circumstance. When the party enters the house they play with a child's set of letters. This gives Frank the opportunity for more provocative teasing. He gives Jane a number of letters from which she has to form a word. She does this and pushes the letters aside. Harriet finds them and forms the word, which is *blunder*. Knightley watches Frank with disgust. Frank gives a word to Emma, then to Jane. The word is *Dixon*, and Jane is obviously angry about it. After Frank and Jane have left, Mr Knightley thinks that it is his duty to warn Emma that Frank is making advances to Jane, but Emma does not take him seriously.

Commentary

Knightley's penetration is, as usual, much more acute than Emma's. The plot clue as to the relationship between Frank Churchill and Jane Fairfax is crystal clear from Frank's slip, and Miss Bates's contribution naively incriminates either herself or Jane as the purveyor of the news. Once more we get the impression that Frank Churchill enjoys these flirtations with danger, but we cannot help feeling that the sufferer every time is Jane Fairfax, who is bent on not giving the game away. The choice of the word *blunder*, a reference to his own slip, shows his daring – and insensitivity – both qualities being observed by Knightley. His giving Emma the word *Dixon* feeds her fantasy about Jane and that man, but of course it embarrasses Jane. Knightley has the pertinacity to question Emma about the word. Her confusion bears testimony to the fact that she has shared a private joke with Frank, but it is more than this. As Knightley goes on to suggest that there is a relationship between Frank and Jane so Emma, confident in the supposed consciousness that Frank is attached to *her*, speaks so definitely to Knightley that he himself begins to be irritated by her.

mother-in-law i.e. stepmother.
Cowper The quotation is from one of Jane Austen's favourite poets, William Cowper (1731–1800), in his poem *The Task*, Book IV, 'The Winter Evening'.
the small-sized Pembroke A table with hinged flaps which can be raised and supported.

Chapter 42

An outing to Box Hill is arranged, but to Emma's dismay Mr Weston asks the Eltons to join the party. The party has to be postponed because of a lame carriage horse, and Knightley proposes a strawberry party instead at Donwell. The idea is taken up by Mrs Elton, who accepts at once and rudely proposes to call it her party, and to invite the guests. Mr Knightley will have none of this. When the party arrives at Donwell, Mrs Weston stays in to look after Mr Woodhouse. The others go out to pick strawberries, though Frank Churchill has not yet arrived. When they rest Mrs Elton tells Jane about a position she has found for her. Jane says she is not ready to accept it, Mrs Elton continues persistent, and Jane in some desperation at this asks Mr Knightley to show them round his gardens. After this walk, with Knightley explaining farming methods to Harriet, they return to the house to eat.

Emma stays with Mr Woodhouse while the others go to see the fish-ponds. Suddenly Jane Fairfax returns to the house in a state of obvious agitation, and asks Emma to tell the others that she has gone home, as it is getting late. Within a quarter of an hour Frank Churchill arrives; he says that he has been detained because Mrs Churchill has had a nervous seizure, and that he has met Jane on the way. He is very hot and irritable, but after he has eaten some food his mood improves. Emma manages to persuade him to stay the night at Donwell, and to join the party to Box Hill the following day.

Commentary

Mrs Elton is much put out by not having a visit from the Sucklings and being thus able to parade their superiorities in Highbury society. On the Box Hill arrangement Emma is mortified by Mr Weston but has to forbear from saying anything to him about his invitation to Mrs Elton. Mr Weston is quite complacent about what he has done. Knightley's half offer of a visit to Donwell is seen by Mrs Elton as a 'proof of intimacy', but he beats her down over the invitation of guests, saying that only one married woman would be allowed to invite what guests she wanted – 'Mrs Knightley'. In fact he stops her from being officious about the arrangements. Emma's re-examination of the Abbey in its loving appraisal contrasts with the verbal excesses and indiscriminate praise of everything by Miss Bates's rival in unpunctuated monotony – Mrs Elton.

Quite a bit of tension is worked up over the non-arrival of Frank, and this is neatly tied in with Jane's worry once Mrs Elton starts to press her about the situation she has found for her. Emma is refreshingly free from any suspicions of Harriet and Knightley when she sees them together, and there is some irony in this since Knightley at the time is the focus of Harriet's attention. Now comes the dramatic climax, or rather two – the sudden entrance and exit of Jane, followed by the perturbed entrance of Frank. Emma feels it fortunate that she is not still in love with him, since he is in such a bad humour. She still does not make the connection with Jane.

Box Hill The author places this seven miles from Highbury.
carte-blanche Freedom of action.

a great set out i.e. elaborate preparations.
al-fresco In the open air (Italian).
neglect of prospect i.e. without the view.
hautboys . . . Chili . . . white wood Each is a type of strawberry.
perfectly answered i.e. been just right.
accomplished i.e. got through.
Madeira A fortified white wine produced in Madeira (in the North
  Atlantic, west of Morocco).

Chapter 43

Emma and Harriet travel together to Box Hill, while the Eltons
take Miss Bates, Jane Fairfax and Mr Knightley, Mr Weston and
Frank Churchill going on horseback. The party splits up into
groups, with Emma and Frank giving the appearance of flirting.
Frank tries to enliven the party by suggesting that each person
should reveal his or her thoughts, but this idea is rejected. He
follows this by announcing that Emma would like each of them
to say one clever thing, or two moderately clever, or three very
dull things. Miss Bates exclaims that the last will suit her well and
Emma, to Miss Bates's chagrin, warns her that she must only say
three things.

After Mr Weston has asked a conundrum, the others beg to be
excused their turns, and the Eltons walk away. Frank ponders
on the fact that the Eltons have found happiness after so short a
time where others might have been less lucky, while Jane argues
that only a weak character would allow an unfortunate acquaint-
anceship to be an inconvenience. Frank says he has no con-
fidence in his own judgement, and asks Emma to find him a
wife. Emma is delighted for, as we know, she has Harriet in
mind. But before the carriages arrive to take them back, Knightley speaks quietly and privately to Emma and reprimands her
for being unkind to Miss Bates. Emma tries to excuse herself,
but she realizes that she is in error, and on the way home she
weeps with mortification.

Commentary

The appraisal of the separation into parties is a form of irony.
Frank, intent perhaps on preserving his secret, is absorbed and
dull at first, but then flirts determinedly, a comment on the
essential selfishness of his character. Emma, however, is

independent of him in her heart. Frank tries to inject life into the group, and offends Mrs Elton by suggesting that Miss Wood-house 'presides'. She finds support for her rejection in her husband, who has by now been reduced to agreement with whatever she says. Frank tactlessly urges what he says Emma wants, and Miss Bates falls into the trap. It is one of the climatic points of the novel: Emma cannot resist her sarcasm, an open offence which shows her lack of tolerance and a temporary insensitivity to Miss Bates. Mr Weston's conundrum is flattering to Emma, and again the Eltons are offended, Mr Elton sneering and referring to himself as 'An old married man'. Frank indulges his sarcasm at their happiness.

Jane's serious contemplation reveals the depths of her feeling, and Frank has recourse to flippancy, probably to hide his own. Knightley's rebuke to Emma shows rightness of judgement and feeling; it also shows an exquisite sensitivity on Miss Bates's account, the fact that she is poor and has lost the comforts she once had. Emma's response once she is alone shows her deeply sympathetic nature. She is not merely conscious of error, she is overcome with anguish and self-criticism at what she has done. This revelation is a masterly stroke – Emma's feelings are now being educated on a much deeper level than hitherto; she is moving towards self-knowledge and humility.

Mickleham 1½ miles north of Box Hill.
Dorking Large town two miles south-west of Box Hill.
Chaperon An older person or married woman who supervises younger women under her charge.
acrostic Lines of writing which form a word, proverb etc.

Chapter 44

Emma is filled with remorse the next day, and goes to the Bateses to make amends for her rudeness on Box Hill. Jane Fairfax is in her room with a headache, but Miss Bates tells Emma that Jane has suddenly decided to accept Mrs Elton's offer of the position of governess to some friends of hers near Bristol. She will be leaving in a fortnight. She also tells Emma that Frank Churchill has returned to Richmond sooner than expected.

Commentary

Emma on the day after is caught in the toils of conscience, though she has already given her father much attention the previous evening, almost by way of consolation and compensation. Ironically, she is interrupted before she can apologize, by the obvious concern and bustle on Jane's account. However, her enquiry about Jane proves to be the way of softening Miss Bates's manner, and Emma feels a genuine access of kindness towards Jane herself. But Emma has to endure Miss Bates's praise of Mrs Elton – 'that good Mrs Elton, whose judgement never fails her' (p.300). Narrative tension is maintained by the announcement of Jane's impending departure *and* the immediately following announcement that Frank has gone. Emma sensitively ponders the difference in the lot of Mrs Churchill and Jane Fairfax, but is dissatisfied with herself in her conscience.

chaise A light, open, horse-drawn carriage, conveying one or two passengers.

Chapter 45

When Emma returns to Hartfield she finds Mr Knightley and Harriet sitting with her father. Knightley gives her a cool welcome, but when he hears that she has been visiting the Bateses he guesses her motive for so doing, takes her hand, and smiles approvingly. Knightley leaves to go to London, where he is to stay with his brother. Emma tells her father the news of Jane, and Mr Woodhouse hopes that she will be happy. Dramatic news of Mrs Churchill's death arrives the next day, Emma believing that this will pave the way for a match between Frank and Harriet. Meanwhile she is anxious to show kindness to Jane Fairfax, but her invitations are declined on the grounds of Jane's ill-health. Emma even takes the carriage to the Bateses, but she meets with no success. She sends arrowroot to Jane, but this too is returned. Later Emma hears that Jane has been seen walking in the meadows on the very afternoon that she had said that she was too ill to take exercise, and this makes her realize that Jane is determined to receive no kindness from her.

Commentary

Emma is certainly moved by her certainty that Mr Knightley has not forgiven her for the incident with Miss Bates. Ironically, her father refers to Emma's constant kindness to the Bateses, and Knightley's warm response even involves the near kissing of Emma's hand, surely an indication of his depth of feeling towards her. Emma's feelings are perfectly conveyed in a series of short sentences that reflect the agitation of her emotions. Emma cunningly diverts her father's concern about Knightley's journey by introducing the news of Jane Fairfax. She succeeds. The next day brings the dramatic news of Mrs Churchill's death, an event which provides the author with ironical commentary: 'Mrs Churchill, after being disliked at least twenty-five years, was now spoken of with compassionate allowances' (p.305). Emma continues in her misguided idea of a match between Frank and Harriet, little suspecting Harriet's real feelings or, for that matter, Frank's. Emma's efforts on Jane's account lead to her humiliation, for she learns that others including Mrs Elton have been admitted. But the report of Jane's wanderings Emma takes as a personal affront, having no inkling of the state of Jane's mind.

express A letter sent by express messenger.

Goldsmith ... when lovely woman stoops to folly Goldsmith was the poet and playwright (1730–74), friend of Dr Johnson. The quotation is from his novel *The Vicar of Wakefield*.

pulmonary complaint Tuberculosis or consumption, disease of the lungs which was the scourge of the nineteenth century.

arrow-root A nutritious starch prepared from the root of the plant of that name, a name derived from the fact that it was originally used as a remedy for wounds caused by poisoned arrows.

Revision questions on Chapters 41–45

1 Describe the various parts played by Mr Knightley in these chapters.

2 In what ways is the visit to Donwell dramatic? You should refer closely to the text in your answer.

3 Describe briefly the visit to Box Hill. What do we learn from it of Emma's character?

4 What incidents in these chapters would lead you to believe that there is an understanding between Frank and Jane?

5 How does Jane Austen maintain narrative tension in these chapters? You may refer to two or three specific incidents in your answer.

Chapter 46

A few days later Mr Weston arrives at Hartfield in some agitation. He asks Emma to go to Randalls to see Mrs Weston, and Emma leaves at once. When she arrives she is told, to her utter amazement, that Frank Churchill has been secretly engaged to Jane Fairfax for about eight months. Mrs Weston is relieved and happy when Emma tells her that she – Emma – is not in love with Frank, though Emma certainly is shaken by Frank's flirtatious behaviour towards her while he was engaged to Jane. She also remembers with some misgiving some remarks that she made to Frank about Jane. Mrs Weston defends Frank and asks Emma not to condemn him or Jane. Emma agrees, and the two of them then convince the anxious Mr Weston that this is a good match for Frank.

Commentary

Note the urgency of the opening of this chapter, raising expectations in the reader's mind. Mrs Weston's restraint only fuels Emma's anxiety – she feels that some disaster has struck her family. Her imagination focuses on Frank and Richmond, but soon she is moved to compassion by the fact of Mrs Weston's looking so ill. The irony is, of course, that she is feeling that Emma will be shocked on her own account by the revelation to come. Emma isn't, but she *is* concerned about this new loss of Harriet's prospects. With commendable frankness Emma puts Mrs Weston out of her misery by asserting that she is not in love with Frank. Mrs Weston's concern – and that of her husband, who cannot face this scene – do credit to them both. Emma reveals her disgust at Frank's past behaviour, not least on Jane's account, but she is won to Mrs Weston's generosity of spirit, discovers that Mr Churchill has given his consent, but broods on the length and complexity of the deception they have all undergone. Emma even agrees, through Mrs Weston's influence, to set

Mr Weston's heart at ease 'and incline him to be satisfied with the match' (p.315). Emma does more than that – she reassures him with her own charm and wit that all is well, and he convinces himself that it was 'the very best thing that Frank could possibly have done' (p.316).

Brunswick Square i.e. where the John Knightleys live – and remember that they are being visited by Knightley himself.

broke **to me** i.e. revealed to me.

Half a dozen natural children perhaps This is Emma's witty imagination at its best – the idea that Mr Churchill may have illegitimate children who could oust Frank from his inheritance is a wickedly fanciful idea on Emma's part.

were offering i.e. were being offered.

On this article i.e. of this particular business (Jane's situation).

Chapter 47

While Emma's anxiety is on account of Harriet and the harm she thinks she has done her by encouraging her to love Frank, she makes herself angry and hurries to Harriet to tell her the news of Frank's engagement. Harriet forestalls her by telling her that she has already heard the news from Mr Weston. To Emma's astonishment, Harriet does not seem in the least put out, and to her further astonishment she learns that the person Harriet has never named but who she does love is Mr Knightley. Emma is horrified and, forced to examine her own feelings, finds that she is in love with Mr Knightley herself. To make things worse, Harriet proceeds to outline the reasons which make her believe that Knightley cares for her, rubbing salt into Emma's wounds by saying that had it not been for Emma's encouragement she herself would never have believed the match with Knightley possible. When Harriet leaves, Emma is distraught, mortified by the thought of the blunders she has made and the self-deception of which she has been guilty. This may lead to her loss of Knightley in what she would regard as a degrading marriage to Harriet.

Commentary

Notice Emma's complete conviction that Harriet will be injured by Frank's love for Jane, and her own willing admission of guilt in encouraging (as she thinks) Harriet's love for him. She is not only riddled with conscience, she is angry at herself. She now thinks that she understands Jane's reactions too – that her offers to Jane were spurned because Jane was jealous of the attentions being paid to her by Frank. Emma, though herself bound to secrecy about Frank, feels that she has an overriding duty to tell Harriet what has happened. Once again, here in moral crisis, Emma's will-power and integrity are pre-eminent.

Harriet's anticipation of what she has to say brings home another truth to Emma – here, as before, she has been wrong. But her education in life experience is to have an even greater chastening with Harriet's admission that she loves Knightley. Moreover, Harriet's comparison of the difference between Knightley and Frank Churchill is precisely, ironically, terribly Emma's own. Harriet, having received Emma's previous encouragement, now unconsciously rubs salt in Emma's wounds by hoping that she will not oppose Harriet's possible match with Knightley – 'But you are too good for that, I am sure' (p.320). The words must be galling to Emma, who suddenly, movingly discovers the state of her own heart. But she is compassionate enough – though fearful – to hear and bear the recital of Harriet's hopes with regard to Knightley. It is a kind of sweet anguish, convincing from Harriet's point of view and hardly less so from Emma's. But when Harriet leaves, Emma has honesty of feeling enough to exclaim 'Oh God! that I had never seen her!' (p.323). There follows a searing examination by Emma of herself and a moving if suffering revelation of her own feelings for Knightley.

rack ... poison Note the strength of these images to convey emotional suffering.
tautology See 'Literary terms' p.5.

Chapter 48

Emma is critical of her own behaviour in the past towards Knightley, her failure to appreciate his advice and his particular goodness. She hopes that Harriet is mistaken and that Knightley will never marry, aware too that she can never marry because of her tie to her father. She writes to Harriet asking her not to come again to Hartfield at the present. Meanwhile Mr and Mrs Weston have paid a visit to Jane, and have found her very distressed at the deception, but when she drives out with Mrs Weston her mood improves and she tells her of her suffering during the secrecy and of her feelings of guilt. Emma is moved to compassion, and regrets having been unkind to her. She faces a grim future, for Mrs Weston is going to have a baby and will not be so readily available as she was, Frank and Jane will no doubt move to Enscombe after their marriage, and Knightley, should he marry Harriet, will no longer be her particular friend. Yet she resolves to try and improve her own conduct.

Commentary

In the depths of her suffering Emma reveals that her love for Knightley would be satisfied, she feels, if only he would be the same as he always has been, in other words always available to advise, comfort, sympathize, be critical but above all be *with* her. She is human enough to wish that Harriet may be wrong and that she will be disappointed. Her extreme sensitivity is shown by her writing to Harriet – she feels that she cannot any further discuss something which injures her so much. There is a neat and moving moral touch in the description of the Bateses' reaction to Jane's engagement and their happiness and gratitude on her behalf. Jane reveals in her narrative to Mrs Weston a capacity for self-blame and of course for suffering. Jane also blames herself for not making allowances for the natural high-spiritedness of Frank. She is also grateful for Emma's kindness to her. Emma is herself so moved by her own situation that she does not listen fully to Mrs Weston. Her capacity for self-pity at the prospect of a changed future is alleviated by her own determination. It seems that she has learned much from these experiences.

tête-à-tête See note p.37.
inquietudes Inward disquiet and distress.

Chapter 49

The following morning, while Mr Perry is with her father, Emma takes a stroll in the garden, where she is joined by Mr Knightley. She is fearful that he will speak of Harriet, and tells him of the engagement between Frank and Jane. He already knows, and is angry with Frank for flirting with Emma when he was already engaged to Jane. He comforts Emma, believing that she is in love with Frank, but Emma tells him that although she enjoyed the flattery of Frank's attentions she has never been in love with him. Mr Knightley seizes his opportunity and proposes to Emma; she is taken completely by surprise, but joyfully accepts.

Commentary

Note that Emma tries to improve her mood by getting out in the air and that it works wonders for her. The tension between herself and Knightley – each unsure of what the other is thinking and feeling – is finely conveyed. Again Mr Weston has provided the information – this time to Knightley – which forestalls Emma's having to announce the news of the Jane–Frank engagement. Knightley's comforting of Emma is exquisitely done, her honesty of response in voicing the truth equally so. We note the warmth between them and the truthful responsibility of Emma's utterance with regard to Frank Churchill: 'It was merely a blind to conceal his real situation with another' (p.335). Knightley is constrained to speak enviously of Frank Churchill, and again Emma misunderstands, thinking that in being somewhat jealous of Frank's future married state he is wishing himself married to Harriet. The misunderstanding is compounded when Emma, out of fear of what he is going to say, tells him not to speak. Knightley, about to propose to her, is mortified, but the proposal is not long delayed. When it comes it is warm, impassioned, tender; Emma is overcome. A delightful authorial reticence speaks for her – 'What did she say? – Just what she ought, of course. A lady always does' (p.338). It is a moving love scene that never spills over into sentimentality. We are reminded throughout it that two people of honesty and integrity are involved.

reprobating Condemning.

Chapter 50

Emma now thinks of the effect her marriage will have on Harriet and on her father, and she decides not to marry while her father is alive. She thinks that it is best to get Harriet away for a while, and she writes arranging for her to stay in London with Isabella. Knightley arrives and, after he leaves, a letter comes from Mrs Weston enclosing a long explanation from Frank Churchill. That letter states that he could not have an open engagement with Jane because of his aunt, and moreover that he flirted with Emma in order to allay suspicion, believing in any case that she would not take him seriously. He sent the piano to Jane, knowing that she would have forbidden it if she had known who had sent it. He is manly enough to emphasize that Jane behaved perfectly throughout the whole deception, and blames himself for the quarrel which started on the day of the visit to Donwell and continued at the Box Hill picnic the next day. This led to him returning to Richmond in a temper, while Jane in her turn impetuously accepted the position obtained for her by Mrs Elton and wrote to Frank breaking off their engagement. This letter reached him on the day his aunt died. He wrote back to Jane at once, but forgot to post the letter. Soon after this Jane returned all his letters and demanded the return of hers, giving her new address at Bristol. Frank realized then what had happened, and at once spoke to his uncle, obtained his permission to marry, and hurried to Highbury to be reconciled to Jane.

Commentary

Emma is very naturally now in a flutter of happiness. Some nice irony plays over Mr Woodhouse's ignorance of what has happened, while Emma feels for him and for Harriet. Once more we note her sense of duty, a sense which would make her put off the marriage while Mr Woodhouse is alive. She also makes provision for Harriet. Such is Emma's conscience and sensitivity on Harriet's account that she cannot bear to see her, writes to her, and enjoys more precious moments in Knightley's company. There follows the arrival of Frank Churchill's letter. Here Jane Austen is employing the technique of conveying information through letters which was so widely used by 18th-century novelists (notably Samuel Richardson, whose novels were written entirely in the form of letters).

Frank's letter reveals the man. He acknowledges his own conceit and his own insistence on secrecy, but his major admission is of being wrong in his attentions to Emma. He bases his justification on Emma's indifference – 'We seemed to understand each other' (p.343) – but the reader is forced to acknowledge that it suits Frank Churchill to say this. He even says that he felt that Emma suspected him, another ironic judgement since for long Emma felt that he was in love with her. It is an impetuous letter, but although there is much self-excuse, the sensitivity of the letter makes the reader, like Emma, inclined not to be too harsh, but to forgive. In some ways it is an anguished letter as Frank relives the quarrel with Jane, and it is significant that he now has little time for Mrs Elton and the part that she has played in his troubles. Note the style of the letter, which exactly reflects the traumatic feelings of Frank Churchill in the short and repetitive sentences.

parley Talk.
caviller One who objects, criticizes.

Revision questions on Chapters 46–50

1 Write an essay on Emma's reactions to the news of Frank Churchill's secret engagement to Jane Fairfax.

2 Consider Emma's reactions to Harriet's news that she (Harriet) is in love with Mr Knightley.

3 In what ways do you consider that Jane Austen makes use of the unexpected in these chapters? You should refer closely to the text in your answer.

4 How far do you sympathize with Frank Churchill in his account of his behaviour as revealed in the letter? Again, you should refer to the text in your answer.

Chapter 51

Emma finishes the letter and forgives Frank. When Knightley arrives she gives it to him to read. Knightley's comments are just, for he accuses Frank of being deceived by his own wishes and of considering little besides his own convenience. He deplores the secrecy and intrigue of the whole affair, but when he has finished the letter he admits that there is no doubt that Frank is really in love with Jane. He hopes that when they are married the influence of Jane will bring about some improvement in Frank's character. Knightley then plans his future with Emma. He accepts the fact that she cannot leave her father, so he asks Emma to let him settle with her at Hartfield when they are married. This will mean that she need not leave her father and Emma, conscious of the sacrifice he is making, promises to think over the proposal. The more she ponders this suggested arrangement, the more she likes it, her only concern now being for Harriet's feelings.

Commentary

When she has finished the letter Emma shows how forgiving she can be; this indicates that she is becoming more tractable. This is probably due to her own happiness with regard to Knightley. Knightley's reading of the letter is punctuated by sound comments, since he himself lives by what he calls 'truth and sincerity'. Knightley comments on the immaturity displayed by Frank in the present of the pianoforte. He also feels that Frank is very verbose, as well as being insensitive to Jane's sufferings. Knightley's practicality now emerges. His scheme for living at Hartfield after their marriage shows his genuine love for Emma – he understands, enters into, and resolves to act upon her relationship with her father in the best possible way. Emma still searches her conscience on this, but is also weighed down by the thought of Harriet's reactions to the loss of Knightley. We note that, in the best possible sense, Knightley and Emma deserve one another – each is capable of integrity, generosity of spirit and altruism, putting the needs of others before self.

Finesse Artfulness.

Chapter 52

Emma is relieved by the fact that Harriet obviously wishes to avoid a meeting, and the arrangement for her to stay with Isabella is concluded. When Emma calls on Jane Fairfax she finds Mrs Elton present, exulting in Jane's secret and presuming that Emma does not know it. Emma is therefore unable to talk to Jane. Mrs Elton awaits her husband's return from a meeting at the Crown with Knightley and others, but Emma points out that the meeting is not to be held until the next day. Mrs Elton contradicts this, but the arrival of her hot and bad-tempered husband confirms that Emma is right. Elton had walked to Donwell to find Knightley but failed to do so, so Emma guesses that Knightley is at Hartfield waiting to see her. She leaves, and on her way utters a few words of encouragement to Jane.

Commentary

Notice how Emma misjudges Harriet's motives and apparent coolness, although in this instance she cannot be expected to know what Harriet is feeling. Again duty motivates Emma and she goes to visit Jane, this time being warmly greeted and noting the great improvement in Jane's looks and manner. Mrs Elton is as ill-bred as ever, folding up a letter which can be finished 'some other time you know', thus displaying her smugness at being in the secret and talking of Mrs S, whom she has appeased, presumably because of the loss of Jane's services. She delights in teasing Emma by referring to Mr Perry as being responsible for Jane's cure. Emma has to endure the fact that 'Mr E is Knightley's right hand' (p.357), but she rides it admirably and is able to see Mrs Elton put down by her own arrogance and incompetence in misjudging the day. Jane reveals that she wishes to confide in Emma, but Elton obtrudes his own sufferings insensitively into the conversation. There is a warm and sympathetic exchange between Emma and Jane.

ridicule In some editions, reticule, a netted handbag.
For when a lady's in the case ... From one of the fables by John Gay (1685–1732), 'The Hare and Many Friends'.
receipt Recipe.

Chapter 53

Mrs Weston has a baby girl. Emma is delighted, while not admitting that the baby may ultimately make a good match for one of Emma's nephews! Harriet seems to be enjoying her stay in London and extends it from a fortnight to a month. John Knightley writes a letter of congratulation to his brother, and Emma is now faced with the necessity of telling her father of the engagement. At first he tries to persuade her against the engagement, mentioning *poor* Isabella and *poor* Miss Taylor, but when Emma points out that having Knightley always there will mean increased happiness for him, he responds to the persuasions of Knightley, Mrs Weston and Isabella, thinking that the marriage could well take place in a year or so. Mr Weston tells Jane this secret, and soon via Miss Bates all Highbury knows and is delighted, except of course the Eltons, who are unpleasantly surprised.

Commentary

Emma's match-making tendencies are revealed as being still alive on the birth of Mrs Weston's daughter. Knightley and Emma have a pleasantly ironic discussion which shows their love for each other and also how fortunate each of them feels in that love. But there is some fine humour in it as well, with Emma hinting that she may call him 'Mr K' in imitation of Mrs Elton's 'Mr E'. Emma feels too sensitive to discuss Harriet with Knightley, but she appreciates Mr John Knightley's letter to her future husband in which he expresses the view that Emma may become worthy of his brother's affection in time. Again this demonstrates Emma's generosity of spirit and her lack of conceit. She also realizes, as she demonstrates to Knightley, that just as his brother will take his part, so her father will take hers. Here she shows a natural wisdom of judgement. Mr Woodhouse's reactions are given faithfully in a series of miserable questions, but the artful persuasion of Knightley and her friends ensures Emma's ultimate success. Mrs Elton's reactions are as indiscriminately vulgar as we would expect.

Madame de Genlis A French writer and educator (1746–1830). She wrote *Adèle et Theodore* in 1782 to illustrate her theories of education.

Chapter 54

Knightley brings the welcome if surprising news to Emma that Harriet is engaged to Robert Martin. Emma will not at first believe it, and Knightley takes her reaction of surprise as reflecting disapproval. But when he assures her of its truth, Emma is delighted, for her conscience is now clear in having accepted Knightley, whereas she had previously believed that Harriet was in love with him. Mr Martin had seen Harriet in London, where he was delivering some papers from Knightley to his brother. He joined the party that evening, dined with them the next day, proposed to Harriet and was accepted. Back at Highbury Mr Woodhouse and Emma drive to Randalls to visit Mrs Weston and the baby; they are surprised to find Frank and Jane there. Overcoming their initial embarrassment, Frank and Emma are soon laughing about the past. Emma feels that she is a friend of Frank's, though she cannot help comparing him with Mr Knightley and rejoicing in the latter's superiority of character.

Commentary

Of all the unexpected occurrences in *Emma*, Knightley's sudden announcement that Harriet is to marry Robert Martin must take pride of place. The fact that Emma takes it shows how far she has come, but in effect it is relief, freedom, joy which condition her response. There is now no need for her to feel any more guilt. She even acknowledges that Knightley knows Harriet as well as she does, and also admits to the foolishness of her judgement in the past. Emma now has an exquisite silence of joy. When they visit Mrs Weston she also has the pleasure of receiving Frank's warm congratulations. He cannot resist recurring to the Perry joke, though, a frailty which perhaps stimulates Emma's comparison of him with Mr Knightley.

Astley's Philip Astley (1742–1814) was the famous equestrian performer and circus-owner. His first circus opened at Westminster in 1770, and he later went on to establish eighteen of them, including Astley's Royal Amphitheatre in London.
drills Agricultural machines for drilling furrows and sowing seed.

Chapter 55

Harriet returns from London, and Emma realizes that she has always favoured Robert Martin. The fact that he has continued to love her despite her refusal has been irresistible to her. Her parentage is revealed, for she is the daughter of a wealthy tradesman who welcomes her engagement. Robert Martin is received at Hartfield, and Emma admits that he is worthy to marry her friend. Harriet and Robert marry in September, Jane goes to stay with the Campbells before her wedding in November, and

Mr Woodhouse is persuaded to agree to Emma and Knightley marrying in October. This comes about because of a number of robberies of poultry yards in the area, a fact that makes Mr Woodhouse welcome the protective presence of his son-in-law.

Commentary

A rounding off of the various marriages. Harriet and her change of mind – although she loved Robert all the time really – cannot be explained, but only put down to human nature. Emma even proves to have been wrong about Harriet's birth! The ending is wise with the recognition of change, and comic with Mr Woodhouse's fears, which actually bring about the wedding he would have tried to put off!

Revision questions on Chapters 51–55

1 How far do you agree with Mr Knightley's comments on Frank Churchill's letter? Refer to the text in your answer.

2 'Mr and Mrs Elton get what they deserve.' Discuss.

3 Explain how Mr Woodhouse is won over to accept his daughter's marriage.

4 Analyse Emma's feelings as they are revealed in these chapters.

Jane Austen's art in *Emma*
The characters

Emma Woodhouse

... handsome, clever, and rich, with a comfortable home and happy disposition ... the power of having rather too much her own way, and a disposition to think a little too well of herself ...

The above mixed quotation is definitive of the character of Emma as she is when we come to know her, but hers is a developing character, capable of change. The novel is really about the education of her feelings, the recognition of error in herself and in relation to others, and the movement towards moral integrity and a kind of humility. And humility is an attribute Emma is far from possessing when first we meet her after the departure of Miss Taylor to become Mrs Weston. Emma is the focal point of the novel, much of the action being seen through her eyes. Most of the situations are the products of her whims and fancies, urged by her wilful nature. The happiness she ultimately finds is the direct result of a change in her character once she has learned the error of her ways.

Emma is nearly twenty-one, the younger daughter of Mr Woodhouse, and heiress to some £30,000. The family is an ancient one; because of the death of her mother when she was young, Emma has been largely brought up by her father and, more particularly, by her governess Miss Taylor. The latter becomes Mrs Weston, and we owe the physical description of Emma to her. It is lyrical and adulatory – 'the true hazel eye ... regular features, open countenance, with a complexion! oh! what a bloom of full health, and such a pretty height and size; such a firm and upright figure ... She is loveliness itself.'

She would appear to be the ideal heroine, but the fact is that Emma is spoiled. She is the cleverest of her family and at the age of ten could answer questions that puzzled her sister at seventeen. She draws and paints well and plays the piano, though she is somewhat dilettante and undisciplined, lacking sustained application. She is generous and charitable: 'the distresses of the poor were as sure of relief from her personal attention and kindness, her counsel and patience, as from her purse.' But while she has a sure sense of moral rightness she undermines this by a capacity for error. Miss Taylor was too mild with her. Emma highly esteemed Miss Taylor's judgement, but was 'directed chiefly by her own'. This is where the essential wilfulness of her character develops. Knightley in fact is her mentor, using a moral yardstick on the girl he has known since she was a child and whom he is later to marry. As he rightly observes, 'ever since she was twelve, Emma has been mistress of the house and of you all', but we must add that she is considerate to her father, defers to him, and is mindful of his comfort.

Emma is, however, always meaning to do what she cannot carry through. When she sketches Harriet we are reminded that she has a portfolio of unfinished portraits; she always meant to read, but never approached the discipline of reading systematically, so that her determination, like that of playing the piano well, never came to anything. She is something of a slave to her whims or what takes her imagination suddenly. Thrown back on her own resources with the departure of Miss Taylor, Emma indulges herself with the idea of match-making on behalf of Harriet. We note at once that she has no conception of the possible consequences of her action. In fact she has too much leisure, too much time for thought, and it must be admitted that she is conscious – though she would not acknowledge it – of exercising patronage. She looks upon Miss Taylor's marriage as a triumph of her own making – 'I planned the match from that hour' and as a result she resolves not to 'leave off match-making'. Emma has no personal vanity. What she does have is the vanity of a person used to getting her own way and growing to think that hers is the only way. With the happy convergence of Harriet Smith and Mr Elton within her Highbury orbit, Emma is able to give full rein to what Mr Knightley calls her 'fancy'.

In implementing a match between Harriet and Mr Elton, Emma shows herself to be blind, snobbish, a manipulator and a very poor judge of character. Although Emma shows her sensitivity at times, with regard to Harriet she is insensitive, letting her whim rule her judgement. Thus it is apparent to the reader that Harriet is very much taken with Robert Martin, and that that young man, highly valued by Mr Knightley, is eminently suitable for her. Emma uses what can best be described as moral blackmail to ensure that Harriet refuses him, feeling that she will 'sink herself forever' in this 'unworthy' connection. A farmer is beneath Emma's social range. She is to learn how wrong, how culpable, how misguided she is.

Emma does everything to further the match with Elton, getting Harriet into the Vicarage, sketching her in front of Mr Elton, playing at riddles with them and interpreting everything as she wants to. She misreads Mr Elton's character and intentions, though she does have occasional doubts about his responses. Those doubts finally catch up with her when Mr Elton, conveniently alone in the carriage with her, proposes to her and denies that he has ever had any interest in Harriet. Emma the snob is, ironically, trapped by Elton the snob. She is angry, surprised, mortified and humiliated; her judgement, her powers of foretelling and influencing have failed. Mr Elton has had 'the arrogance to raise his eyes to her', which shows the nicety of Emma's sense of breeding and status. Yet it is a great tribute to her resilience and a certain unselfishness in her nature that she is not so much concerned for herself as for Harriet and the hurt this will cause her. If only, she feels, 'could the effects of her blunders have been confined to herself'. She takes consolation from the fact that Mr Elton was not really in love with her (he soon marries on the rebound). She is repentant, acknowledges her foolishness in trying to bring two people together and is particularly kind and sympathetic to Harriet. She resolves to be 'humble and discreet, and repressing imagination all the rest of her life'.

But Emma, being Emma, cannot do so. Her life continues full of misguided speculation and a capacity for misjudgement. With the arrival of Frank Churchill and her getting to know him Emma's imagination takes new flight. She enjoys the fact that she and Frank are 'coupled in their friends' imagination' (though of course she has earlier resolved never to marry) and she convinces herself that Frank intends to be closely acquainted with her; in fact, that he is courting her and is well on the way to being in love with her. Eventually she is convinced that he is about to propose to her (he is probably about to confide in her about Jane) and she forms 'a thousand schemes for the progress and close of their attachment' even 'inventing elegant letters'. She is, of course, wrong about Frank, who is using her as a cover for his clandestine affair with Jane. She fantasizes about her relationship with Frank, sometimes imagining that she is in love, at others finding it strange that she should not be moved by his absence. She is very taken with his company, so much so that she occasionally forgets herself, as in the celebrated rudeness to Miss Bates for which she is reprimanded by Mr Knightley.

Emma is always aware of Mr Knightley and his views, from his dislike of her attitude towards Harriet and Robert Martin to his constant criticism of the shallowness of Frank Churchill. It is part of Emma's education that she should come to know of her real feelings for Knightley through her own misguided judgements about his relationship with Harriet and with Jane. She is obviously somewhat irked by Knightley's respect and liking for Jane – after all, Jane is more accomplished than Emma is – but is very relieved to find that he doesn't consider her in the light of a wife. She obstinately refuses to see that Knightley's kindness to Harriet is responsible for the latter's ambitions with regard to him, ambitions which she unwittingly encourages because she thinks Harriet is really thinking of Frank Churchill. Misguided here, she even imagines that Jane Fairfax is in love with Mr Dixon for saving her life, when of course all Jane's energies are concentrated on preserving the secrecy of her relationship with Frank.

Yet Emma changes despite this wilful need to manage or at least to be in the know with regard to other people's lives. She is self-analytical, acknowledges error, vows to improve, and genuinely tries to do so. Consider her concern for Harriet being hurt again, this time over Knightley, her visit to Miss Bates the day after Box Hill in order to apologize, her attempts to help Jane in her anguish, attempts which she repeats despite their rejection. She has a degree of self-honesty and a capacity to be generous. One feels that nature and nurture combine to spoil Emma, but that because of her resilience and enlightenment she turns error in herself to advantage, not self-advantage but advantage in the sense that she *learns* from her mistakes and her learning benefits others.

Mrs Weston calls Emma 'an excellent creature'. It is perhaps too distant an observation, for Emma is not lacking in warmth. She is always on edge about her father's needs, heading off inflammatory remarks from Mr John Knightley, for example. She is a true heroine, because she comes to humility and self-recognition through suffering. She always has moral awareness, and knows when she offends; she learns social awareness, and recognizes in Robert Martin the kind of genuineness that characterizes his landlord. Emma's is not a sudden reformation, it is an awakening through the long influences of Mr Knightley to rightness of judgement and action. This is no lukewarm conditioning, for Emma is sprightly, spirited, witty, and may be expected to challenge Knightley as well as listen to him. At the end of the book, Emma claims she is not a match-maker, refusing to acknowledge that she has any idea of 'making a match' for Mrs Weston's baby daughter 'hereafter, with either of Isabella's sons'. This is Emma's saving grace throughout; she is always able to laugh at herself. She suffers from no traces of idealization, and the result is a heroine who is psychologically true to herself and to life, her blemishes like our own and her good qualities the result of experience and endeavour.

Mr Knightley

a sensible man about seven or eight-and-thirty . . . one of the few people who could see faults in Emma Woodhouse, and the only one who ever told her of them.

Knightley (we hardly, if ever, think of him being called George) is the owner of Donwell Abbey with its home farm. He is also a magistrate, a tall, active man with a fine upright figure and an alert mind, possessing excellent social, moral and practical judgement. He is good-natured and much respected locally. Mr Elton looks up to him and is very pleased to think, and to say, that Knightley is his friend. Mr Martin, his tenant, comes to ask his advice about marriage, and he is always seen to good advantage. He is generous of his time and service, seeing to it that the utmost respect is accorded to Miss Bates and Jane Fairfax – we remember that he sends his carriage to fetch them to the Coles' dinner. He also sends the Bateses presents from his farm, enduring the vociferous thanks of Miss Bates and her unrelated ramblings with politeness and fortitude. Without being officious or insensitive, he is watchful of behaviour in others, particularly in Emma. He notices that Mr Elton snubs Harriet and, though not a dancing man himself, quickly comes to her rescue by dancing with her, to Emma's delight.

He is mindful of Jane Fairfax's health, considering it selfish and inconsiderate of Frank Churchill to insist on another song from Jane at the Coles' dinner. He offers Donwell Abbey as a substitute visit for Box Hill, despite the fact that it is Mrs Elton who is to the fore, and he prevents her from issuing her own invitations on his behalf. In fact he can be very firm when he wants to, though generally he is all kindness and consideration. He is always solicitous of Mr Woodhouse's well-being (note particularly his providing for him during the Donwell Abbey visit) and this helps to facilitate his marriage with Emma.

His logical, forthright mind forms an excellent contrast to Emma's illogical flights of fancy. When Emma befriends Harriet – or rather, takes her over – he sees at once that the liaison will harm both girls. His views are soon put to the test. Seeking to raise Harriet above her station, Emma virtually causes her to reject Robert Martin, since she has more socially ambitious plans for Harriet in the person of the smoothly egotistical Mr Elton. Mr Knightley is thoroughly indignant when he hears this and upbraids Emma with his usual forthrightness – 'You saw her answer – you wrote her answer too. Emma, this is your doing' (Chapter 8). Now this is accurate and strong, both qualities of Knightley's character, and Emma is somewhat chastened though not put off by its force. Moreover, Knightley is a very clear reader of character, and tells Emma that Mr Elton is certainly aiming higher than Harriet. Events prove him right in the social sense, though arguably Elton deserves the wife he gets.

Knightley is so often right that there is every chance that the reader could see him as a prig. It is a measure of Jane Austen's creative and imaginative genius that Knightley, like Emma, runs true to himself and true to life. There is no suggestion that he is too good to be true, though there is every indication in his statements that he is too true to be unequivocally good. Although Knightley triumphs over Emma in relation to Mr Elton, he is far too naturally well-bred to refer to it. Knightley in fact has some telling silences in other parts of the novel, indicative of his displeasure. But, and this is the mark of the man, he always responds generously to any sympathetic approach, as he does when he and Emma are with his brother's children.

There is a nice balance struck with Emma. She feels apprehensive on Knightley's account with Jane Fairfax and with Harriet – his interest in them helps her to know her own heart. And Knightley is certainly jealous of her interest in Frank Churchill. He dislikes superficiality, the easy familiarity which stamps Frank Churchill as the fashionably gregarious man. Consequently, with Emma the apparent focus of Frank's attentions, he displays some edgy jealousy. He calls Frank a 'trifling, silly fellow' when he learns that he has been to London for a haircut, and even when he is able to go through Frank's letter in the knowledge that he, Knightley, has Emma, he still reflects that he would have distrusted Frank even had Emma not been involved.

Knightley's disapproval of all the trouble taken to have the Ball at the Crown is another reflection of his jealousy, but it is also a reflection of his age – Knightley is a sober, older man who takes his responsibilities seriously. Again, this must not be construed as dullness. There is nothing more sensitive in the whole of the novel than Knightley's proposal to Emma – it is full of uncertainty, fear, modesty and humility, as well as the obvious expression of his love for her. Such is his delicacy of feeling that we see him loving her throughout the previous years without giving expression to that love for fear of offence. Although he is her mentor, there is no need to think of any inequality in their relationship. Knightley has a quiet humour of his own to balance Emma's natural vivacity and playfulness. His integrity and moral perspective are alike impeccable, and he has the quality of sincerity that brings character alive in fiction.

Frank Churchill

She believed he was reckoned a very fine young man.

Frank Churchill, Mr Weston's son, was adopted by his uncle and aunt, Mr and Mrs Churchill, on the death of his mother when he was only two. When he comes of age he assumes the Churchills' name and becomes heir to their fortune. There is much speculation about Frank before we, the readers, meet him, or indeed before any of the Highbury characters meet him either. He has not made a point of visiting his father very soon after the latter's marriage, and this throws some doubt on his character, fuelled by Knightley's suggestion that he has wasted his time at the 'idlest haunts in the kingdom', watering places.

When Emma meets Frank she finds him very good-looking, charming, naturally fluent, spirited, lively and well-bred. He enjoys being sociable, puts himself out to make a good impression, and knows exactly what to say in order to make himself pleasant and accepted – hence his praise of Mrs Weston to Emma. But we should not forget one thing. When Frank first appears in Highbury he is already, unknown to anyone else, secretly engaged to Jane Fairfax. This puts an additional strain on his behaviour and indeed explains much of it. This is not apparent to his father's friends and certainly not to his father; Emma even considers that he has 'all the life and spirit, cheerful feelings, and social inclinations' of that father.

Frank's whim of going to London to get his hair cut, while it provokes the condemnation of Mr Knightley, raises some doubts in other minds, notably Emma's, about him. Of course his real reason for going – to buy the piano, which is sent to Jane – is not revealed, so that Emma suspects him of 'vanity, extravagance, love of change, restlessness of temper' and, in fact, these are strangely true in view of his concealment. We must also take account of the author's irony at the figure he cuts – he is so much liked and appreciated that people forgive 'the little excesses of such a handsome young man – one who smiled so often and bowed so well'. Both these last comments in fact reveal the strain Frank is under – he is constantly aware that he must keep up his act.

Frank's appropriation of Emma, his determined flirting with her – which he later says he knew she would accept for what it was – shows that he is inherently selfish. He is using Emma to lull any suspicions of his feelings for Jane. Knightley's stricture of him comes to mind, that he is 'always deceived in fact by his own wishes and regardless of little besides his own convenience'. Even the secrecy with Jane is selfish since he knows that Mrs Churchill would never agree to the match, and he will not run the risk of being disinherited. There is some subtlety in his presentation in relation to Jane: he criticizes her yet cannot keep away from her; probably enjoys the flirting with Emma as a way of provoking a positive response from Jane; delights in teasing Jane – the children's alphabet game (forerunner of 'Lexicon' and later 'Scrabble'?) is particularly revealing here – and undoubtedly contributes much towards making Jane ill. He certainly provokes her into taking the situation which Mrs Elton is so anxious she should have.

Emma notes Frank's moodiness, and the reader is forced to ask, if he is capable of treating Jane with such a degree of insensitivity, what hope does this hold out for a happy marriage? There is a certain instability about him, but I suppose we must accept, as Emma does and Knightley in part does, the explanations and apologies of the letter he writes to Mrs Weston after he has obtained his uncle's consent to the marriage to Jane. Again we note the timing. What would have happened if that consent – and presumably the prospect of his inheritance – had been withheld? Emma is aware of Frank's sufferings and also of how much in love he is with Jane. He is, however, a very selfish young man; Knightley's hopes are more idealistic than real, but perhaps we should let him have the last say on Frank Churchill:

He has had great faults, faults of inconsideration and thoughtlessness; and I am very much of his opinion in thinking him likely to be happier than he deserves: but still as he is, beyond a doubt, really attached to Miss Fairfax, and will soon, it may be hoped, have the advantage of being constantly with her, I am very ready to believe his character will improve, and acquire from hers the steadiness and delicacy of principle that it wants. (Chapter 51)

Jane Fairfax

her temper excellent in its power of forebearance, patience, self-control; but it wants openness.

Mr Knightley's words quoted above are a great relief to Emma, who at this point feels that she can never really make a friend of Jane Fairfax; she resents her the more when Mrs Weston puts forward the idea that Knightley is interested in Jane. She is an orphan, for her father was a soldier who died in action and her mother died of grief soon after. Adopted by her grandmother and aunt at the age of three, she was fortunately befriended and helped by Colonel Campbell and his wife, the Colonel having had a great regard for Jane's father. Their only daughter became so friendly with Jane that at the age of nine she was virtually re-adopted by the Campbells, thereafter visiting Highbury at irregular intervals. Jane is very elegant, with beautiful features, deep grey eyes, dark eyelashes, and a clear delicate skin. She has had a good education, is a person of some talent and ability, and is fully qualified in every way to begin her career as a governess.

But in spite of these advantages, Emma, as we have seen, does not really like her, for she finds Jane cold and reserved. Strangely, Emma stumbles, for once, on the truth – 'I have no reason to think ill of her ... except that such extreme and perpetual cautiousness of word and manner ... is apt to suggest suspicions of there being something to conceal.' Of course there is, and Jane's manner becomes more self-consciously distant because of the position in which she has been placed by Frank. She suffers considerably, and Emma has feeling (and humour) enough to pity her because of the constant barrage of words she has to put up with from Miss Bates.

Jane's real suffering, however, is seen in her unsatisfactory interactions with Frank as he keeps up his determined flirtation with Emma (Jane obviously resents this) *and* makes a number of references to Weymouth and their secret relationship. She has very little relief from the tensions of the situation – one quiet conversation with Mr John Knightley apart – and she is badgered towards a governess's post by the insensitive and voluble Mrs Elton, who takes her up very obviously as a counterbalance to Emma. Jane therefore has little if any peace of mind; at home her garrulous aunt, in society the prospect of Mrs Elton or of Frank flirting with Emma. It is no wonder that the pressure gets to her, and that the visit to Donwell Abbey precipitates a crisis in Jane's unhappy mind. Frank is so late coming from London that she has already left Donwell. They meet on the road and, though we don't know what is said, there is obviously some kind of quarrel, seen from Frank's bad temper (which Emma is somewhat put out by) when he arrives. The Box Hill party is no better, with Frank's ostentatious flirting with Emma even worse. The next day we are told that Jane is ill and that she has accepted a post as governess to a friend of Mrs Elton. She is ill for some days, overcome by the strain of her life of deception, and rejects Emma's overtures of friendship and help.

The death of Mrs Churchill effectively removes the obstacle to Frank's marriage with Jane. His letter to Mrs Weston spells out the nature of Jane's suffering and the ever-present torture of her conscience. She says that 'Pain is no expiation. I never can be blameless' (Chapter 48). This scrupulous morality contrasts favourably with the irresponsibility of her fiancé who had placed her in an intolerable position. Jane is particularly warm to Emma when all is revealed, and we feel that Emma, the somewhat changed and chastened Emma, will come to like her in the end. Jane is seen almost always in adversity, but we note the struggle for integrity and openness which her situation – and in part her health – deny her for much of the action of the novel.

Harriet Smith

Harriet certainly was not clever, but she had a sweet, docile, grateful disposition; was totally free from conceit; and only desiring to be guided by any one she looked up to.

At the end of the novel we learn that Harriet Smith is the natural daughter of a well-to-do London tradesman. She was early placed at Mrs Goddard's school in Highbury. When the novel opens she is seventeen years old, has risen in the school from scholar to parlour-boarder and is very pretty, with 'blue eyes, light hair, regular features, and a look of great sweetness' (Chapter 3). Emma, with too much leisure on her hands, meets Harriet at a card party at Hartfield and, admiring her prettiness and docile disposition, decides to make a companion of her. Unfortunately she also decides to find a husband for Harriet, who, naive, inexperienced, looking up to 'Miss Woodhouse', allows herself to be easily led and influenced by Emma. 'Her character depends upon those she is with' observes Knightley, and since she is constantly in Emma's company she is conditioned to believe what Emma says. Knightley fears that Emma will give Harriet ideas above her station in life, and this is precisely what occurs. Harriet, who is attracted to Robert Martin and has appreciated the kindness of his family, rejects his proposal of marriage virtually on Emma's insistence because he is only a farmer. This reflects her youth and inexperience and too great pliability; it is quite obvious from her reactions that she *would* have accepted the proposal if she had not met Emma.

Harriet is childishly amazed when Emma tells her (erroneously) that Mr Elton is in love with her, and the immature and romantic quality of her own 'love' for Elton is shown in her collecting a small piece of sticking plaster that Mr Elton had touched and the end of an old pencil he had used. Her innocence and lack of worldliness are shown in the encounter with the mob of gipsies, where she naively offers them a shilling to leave her alone. Only the timely arrival of Frank Churchill saves her from the consequences of such folly. But although she is ingenuous and ignorant and suffers much from the power of Emma's personality and her superior status, she displays self-control, humility, and a very Christian sense of forgiveness. When, fully believing that Mr Elton is in love with her, she hears that he has proposed to Emma and that the whole affair has been a gross mistake on Emma's part, she takes the news well and blames nobody. She is generously full of praise for Mr Elton's bride and wishes the couple well with all her heart. Later, when Mr Elton rudely snubs her at the ball, she bears no grudge, hoping that he and his wife will be happy together and 'it will not give me another moment's pang' (Chapter 40). She has little judgement, but certainly no malice.

Mr Knightley, who comes to Harriet's rescue after the snub and earns her gratitude and (temporarily) her love, revises his opinion of her, saying that she is 'an artless, amiable girl, with very good notions, very seriously good principles', and Emma herself appreciates her tenderness of nature. She comes to value Harriet for what she is rather than what she thought she could make of her. We feel it right and consistent that Harriet should marry Robert Martin, but it would undermine Jane Austen's concept of character if Harriet did not display some weakness. She does. She is impressionable and very young in attitude, going from love for Mr Elton to love for Knightley, the latter being perhaps almost a father in place of the father she doesn't know. But she gets over both very quickly, which may indicate some shallowness of nature. Yet if we remember that Robert Martin was her first love, then her marrying him would seem to be the natural corrective to the superficial nature of much of her feelings under Emma's tutelage.

Mr Elton

Full of his own claims, and little concerned about the feelings of others.

Mr Elton is a subtle study in egoism, a reflection of Jane Austen's notation of the difference between appearance and reality in the human personality. The vicar of Highbury is generally thought of as a handsome young man, well-meaning, respectable; and Emma finds him initially good-humoured. He sighs and studies 'for compliments' rather too much for her liking, and his manner is over-elegant, as in the scene where Emma paints Harriet, where he flatters and propitiates Emma almost beyond reason. He is 'in continual raptures', all reflecting a kind of insincerity and superficiality, though one must be fair and say that at this stage he fancies himself in love with Emma. She thinks him, ironically, 'almost too gallant to be in love', interpreting everything he does – like going to get the frame, for instance – as being for Harriet. But Knightley, whose good sense is unques-

tionable throughout, knows his man; he sees that Elton is mercenary; that he will 'talk sentimentally, but he will act rationally'
(Chapter 8). He also asserts that Elton is conceited and vain, and
that he is very conscious of status – he is a snob. All this is proved
true by events.

For a moment when he makes passionate advances to Emma
he commands our compassion, for he is not entirely at fault in
believing that she has encouraged him. But his protestations
make him appear ridiculous: he is 'hoping – fearing – adoring –
ready to die if she refused him' (Chapter 15). Of course he
doesn't die, though he is at first injured, then disillusioned and
finally angry. He obviously looks down on Harriet, and is little
concerned for the feelings of others. It is noticeable that after his
rejection his inherent vulgarity, insensitivity, selfishness and
general unattractiveness assert themselves. He is hardly the Mr
Elton Emma thought she knew or even the one we have come to
know. He is conceited indeed, for he has got what he wants, an
heiress who will ensure that he no longer need be dependent on
dining out. He is, one is forced to admit, hardly a Christian in
the true sense of the word. Engaged to Miss Augusta Hawkins,
he flaunts his self-satisfaction in Highbury before returning with
his insufferable bride. His pride in her reflects his want of taste
and his shallowness. He and his wife sneer at Harriet and treat
her with contempt; at the ball at the Crown he slights Harriet by
refusing to dance with her, and then exchanges smiles of complacent satisfaction with his wife. There is also the implication
that although he and his wife deserve each other in the worst
possible sense, they may not be altogether happy, mainly
because each lacks the capacity to give and each lacks that pre-
requisite of moral stability – sincerity.

Mrs Elton

Self-important, presuming, familiar, ignorant, and ill-bred.

Miss Augusta Hawkins is the younger daughter of a Bristol
merchant. She marries the Rev. Philip Elton after a brief
courtship and comes to live at Highbury. There is much speculation about her, and she has a dowry of 'so many thousands that
would always be called ten', but Emma shrewdly notes that her
only claim to social distinction is her brother-in-law Mr Suckling
who keeps two carriages. She is not unattractive in features but

she has no elegance of voice or manner to recommend her. Emma's soon-to-be-formed opinions are borne out – Mrs Elton is vain, self-satisfied, self-important, pushing, intent on being seen to be superior, 'but with manners which had been formed in a bad school, pert and familiar' (Chapter 32). She talks incessantly – usually about her brother-in-law's residence at Maple Grove, which she regards as the model of social status and excellence. She boasts of his barouche-landau among other things, and of her own accomplishments, which are nonexistent. She affects to be independent of society, but in fact she is parasitic on it, feeding her vanity by condescending; preening herself and generally talking inflated nonsense to the limited captive audiences of Highbury who initially pay court to her. She delights in being first everywhere as a married woman, thus usurping Emma's past pre-eminence. She comes to Highbury intent on being patronizing from her superior worldly position. She does her best to take over Emma at first, suggesting that they form a music club; recommends Bath for Mr Woodhouse's health, and infuriates Emma by saying that she can give her letters of introduction to the best society there. Mrs Elton is always centre stage, seeming to think that the Ball at the Crown is in her honour, and thus welcoming the guests. When Knightley offers the strawberry picking at Donwell she tries to take it over as her party and to invite the guests, but Knightley is equal to her presumption and her arrogance.

She is familiar, referring to Mr Knightley as Knightley and her husband as 'Mr E', and she is astonished to find that Mrs Weston, Emma's late governess, is so ladylike. She aids and abets her husband's slighting of Harriet, and determines to take Jane Fairfax under her wing once she realizes that Emma will not be manipulated by her (Mrs Elton). It may well be that she also feels that it is difficult to maintain her superiority in Emma's presence; she may even be jealous of Emma. She is, as Emma says, 'A little upstart, vulgar being ... all her airs of pert pretension and underbred finery' (Chapter 32).

Mr Woodhouse

a valetudinarian all his life, without activity of mind or body, he was a much older man in ways than in years; and though everywhere beloved for the friendliness of his heart and his amiable temper, his talents could not have recommended him at any time.

This quotation spells out the way of life and the temperament of Mr Woodhouse. He is loved, respected, perpetually worried about his own health and diet and that of others. He has set habits, regular friends, and does not wish to depart in any way from a pattern of activity that involves change; thus he deplores the fact that '*poor* Miss Taylor' has just become Mrs Weston, and so has left Hartfield for Randalls. His mind cannot take in that she wishes to do so; the loss, he feels, is hers, but in reality he knows that the loss is his.

Mr Woodhouse has a nervous disposition, easily becoming depressed, 'fond of everybody that he was used to, and hating to part with them'. In fact, as has been indicated above, he hates change of all kinds. His only exercise is a walk in the garden, planned according to season, but never extending beyond the shrubbery. He has a horror of late hours and dinner parties. The ball proposed at the Crown Inn finds him worried about damp rooms and draughts. He has a fire at Hartfield practically every night of the year, and when he goes to Donwell Abbey in June Knightley thoughtfully provides one for him there. It would be true to say that he regards Mr Perry the apothecary as an authority on his particular needs and by analogy the needs of everyone else.

His worries on behalf of others often focus on diet. He himself takes very simple food – thin gruel, a lightly boiled egg – and has a horror of anything as rich as wedding cake. He is the recipient of the author's irony because of his foibles – 'while his hospitality would have welcomed his visitors to everything, his care for their health made him grieve that they would eat.' He is equally concerned about the weather and the danger of venturing out for his family and friends, anxious to know whether Frank Churchill has escaped catching cold on his journey, and asking Jane Fairfax after her trip to the post office in the rain whether she has changed her stockings. He is a good if irritating old man, and he is touched with a kind of pathetic humour throughout. John Knightley from time to time voices irritation with him, and we more fully understand Emma's need to escape into her own fantasies when we realize how much of her time is taken up in seeing to her father. Crotchety he certainly is, but he never loses our sympathy or our interest. He has the recognizable traits of the old, strongly individualized in a kind of quavering and solicitous persistence.

Miss Bates

She was a great talker upon little matters.

Miss Bates, like Mr Woodhouse, is a delightful character, who provides much of the humour of the novel and who, like Mr Woodhouse, can also be irritating. She lives on a small income and devotes herself to the care of her mother. She is popular because she has a 'universal good-will and contented temper which worked such wonders. She loved everybody, was interested in everybody's happiness, quick-sighted to everybody's merits ... The simplicity and cheerfulness of her nature, her contented and grateful spirit, were a recommendation to everybody and a mine of felicity to herself' (Chapter 3). Here we note the irony mixed with the commendation. She is, it must be admitted, a gossip, and this endears her to Mr Woodhouse, who includes her in his 'second set' of card players. Miss Bates suffers from the need to keep talking at all times – she wanders from topic to topic without any apparent sense of direction, though certain pivotal interests – like her niece Jane – obviously come in for the lion's share of her random verbosity. She pauses only to take breath, yet she is kind, concerned, considerate, her comparative poverty ensuring consideration in return from those who are well-bred. Hence Emma's realization, reinforced by Knightley's reprimand, of the injury she has caused poor Miss Bates by her flippant wit at Box Hill. It is to Miss Bates's credit that although she appears a little cooler when Emma visits her the next day, she soon responds to Emma's warmth, making no reference to the previous day's incident. She forgives and forgets, the pressing news of the moment cancelling all else.

Her lack of conversational discrimination provides genuine humour. Take this opening mixed gambit at Hartfield from Chapter 21:

'Oh! my dear sir. How are you this morning? My dear Miss Woodhouse – I am quite overpowered. Such a beautiful hind-quarter of pork. You are too bountiful! Have you heard the news? Mr Elton is going to be married.'

Perhaps her choicest monologue is addressed to Emma on her way to inspect Jane's piano. It is quite breathless, lasts about five minutes with only one break, and ranges over a number of subjects including the piano and a rivet in her mother's spectacles, the kitchen chimney, baked apples, the Wallises' bread,

Jane's appetite, apple dumplings, ribbons, gloves, Frank Churchill, Mr Woodhouse, and a tale about Mr Knightley, William Larkins and a basket of apples. Even at the Ball she only stops talking in order to eat. Although she provides amusement for the listener, her non-stop talking would certainly tax the stamina of her listeners. There is little doubt that it taxes the stamina of the already undermined Jane Fairfax so much that she finds Mrs Elton tolerable by comparison. Not that anyone, Emma apart, is unkind to Miss Bates. Emma's is the only acidic valuation of the innocent, harmless, garrulous lady when she observes she is 'so silly – so satisfied – so smiling – so prosing – so undistinguishing and unfastidious.' Here the punctuation itself is a parody of Miss Bates's manner, but Emma is later to offer a revision which I think we may accept, of her earlier judgement: 'I know there is not a better creature in the world: but you must allow, that what is good and what is ridiculous are most unfortunately blended in her.'

Mrs Weston

A sweet-tempered woman and a good wife.

Miss Taylor as she was had lived at Hartfield for sixteen years as governess to Mr Woodhouse's two daughters. There is little doubt that by letting Emma have her own way she has contributed greatly to her being spoiled, but she is an intelligent, gentle, well-informed woman, and 'the mildness of her temper had hardly allowed her to impose any restraint'. Although Emma – and more particularly Mr Woodhouse – deplore the 'loss' of Miss Taylor on her marriage, they have little need to do so. Visits between Randalls and Hartfield are a daily occurrence.

Mrs Weston, as she now is, is very concerned to treat her stepson Frank Churchill well, and Emma imagines her anxiety to please him on his first visit. She assumes a well-meaning proprietary interest in him, ready to defend him from criticism from beginning to end. This may in fact show a degree of sensitivity beyond what she is given credit for – she may be covering up his shortcomings on her husband's account. We particularly remark her kindness to Mr Woodhouse, and she is always considerate to him, as we note from the way she puts herself out to be with him at the Donwell visit. She is a little disconcerted by the arrangements for the ball at the Crown when she has inspected the accommodation, but soon adjusts to the influence and suggestions of others without losing any face. There is little doubt that Mrs Weston is sincerely and deeply attached to Emma, and we suspect that she has some match-making in mind with regard to Emma and Frank Churchill. Well-bred and consistently sensible, she has no weakness and obviously delights in motherhood and, once she realizes that there has been no attachment between Emma and Frank, rejoices in the love-match between Emma and Knightley.

Mr Weston

A good-humoured, pleasant, excellent man.

Mr Weston was born in Highbury, received a good education and, inheriting a small legacy, joined the county militia. His cheerful disposition had soon made Captain Weston a popular officer and, when he met Miss Churchill of a great Yorkshire family he married her despite the objections of her family. But the marriage was not a success because, despite his 'warm heart and sweet temper' his wife regretted the loss of her former luxuries and they lived beyond their income. Mrs Weston died after three years, leaving her husband with a child to provide for and in much poorer circumstances than he had been used to. The boy – Frank – was adopted by Weston's brother-in-law. Captain Weston left the militia and entered trade; after twenty years he had made sufficient money to purchase an estate in Highbury, to marry Miss Taylor, and to live like a country gentleman. He shows that he has a pleasant, sociable nature but occasionally he is guilty of too much open-heartedness – when he invites Emma to inspect the arrangements at the Crown for the ball she finds that he has invited several other people too. He is chatty, convivial; inordinately proud of Frank; spreads the news of Emma's engagement; is cheerfully optimistic at all times.

Mr John Knightley

He was not a great favourite with his sister-in-law.

The younger brother of George Knightley 'was a tall, gentlemanlike and very clever man; rising in his profession, domestic, and respectable in his private character; but with reserved manners which prevented his being generally pleasing;

and capable of being sometimes out of humour' (Chapter 11).

Emma's attitude is conditioned by the fact that John Knightley is not as patient with his father-in-law as Emma would have wished. He is somewhat unsociable and expresses his discontent at dining at Randalls when he could so easily have stayed at home. He has a low opinion of social conversation, stigmatizing it by the word 'dull'. He takes a rather spiteful pleasure in telling Mr Woodhouse of the snow, thus casting doubts on whether they will be able to get home from Randalls. He has a somewhat cynical view of life, encapsulated in the phrase 'business, you know, may bring money, but friendship hardly ever does.' He is kind in a rather bluff way and enjoys talking to Jane Fairfax, probably feeling that she is something of a kindred soul. He is shrewd, warning Emma that Mr Elton is interested in her rather than in Harriet.

Isabella Knightley

A devoted wife, a doting mother.

Emma's elder sister is 'a pretty, elegant little woman ... remarkably amiable and affectionate; wrapt up in her family' (Chapter 11). She resembles her father in the sense that she is over-anxious about her own health and that of her children, but she is basically benevolent. She is alarmed at the fall of snow while they are staying at Randalls, and imagines herself cut off from the children. Unlike Emma, she is not an intelligent woman but is happy to pass her life quietly, praising those she likes, appreciating their good qualities and constantly doting on them but unaware of their faults, and always innocently occupied.

Robert Martin

Good sense and good principles.

He has sound judgement and is open and straightforward, and Knightley speaks very well of him. He continues to love Harriet, who has only rejected him because Emma has persuaded her that she should not marry a mere farmer. Ironically, and because of Emma, he is thrown together with Harriet in London. Her feelings for him are re-kindled and they marry, to the delight of Knightley and the revised acceptance of Emma.

Other characters not mentioned here should be examined for

their major traits and their truth to life. Note that we never see Mrs Churchill, Mr Dixon or Colonel Campbell, but that they are brought into the action by retrospect and we feel that we know them. This is one of the major facets of Jane Austen's art in *Emma*.

Style

Jane Austen's style has many facets, and all subserve the disciplines of her art. She admired the eighteenth-century poets like Cowper, and she also admired Dr Johnson. Both are the masters of the measured phrase, and Jane Austen is the mistress of it too. She writes always with superb economy, with no wasted words; unlike Miss Bates, who wastes her words by running and rambling on, Jane Austen knows exactly when to stop and when to continue. With Miss Bates she continues, because Miss Bates cannot be stopped once she is in full flood. In *Emma* the style is the character; so individualized is the conversation of Jane Austen's characters that we would not mistake the delivery and the sentiments of Mr Elton for those of Knightley, nor Knightley's for Elton's or Frank Churchill's. Nor could we confuse Emma's with Jane Fairfax's; nor Miss Bates's with Mrs Elton's, though their verbosity is similar. The differences are marked; Mrs Elton is conscious of condescension, Miss Bates is desirous only of pleasing.

It is easy to see why Jane Austen's style is so modern, and we use the word 'modern' here to signify clarity, immediacy, ready comprehension on the part of the reader. Jane Austen's language stands the test of time; it is as alive now as it was in her own time, even allowing for different shades of meaning in some words. No modern script-writer needs to adapt Jane Austen for the stage or television. Her dialogue is natural, meaningful, crisp. When Emma says,

'I saw her answer, nothing could be clearer.'

and Knightley replies,

'You saw her answer! You wrote her answer too. Emma, this is your doing. You persuaded her to refuse him.'

what we are aware of is the emotional temperature of the speakers as revealed by their language. Emma is essentially honest, Knightley is forthright to the point of bluntness when he has to be. Both characters are evident from their words.

When a niece of Jane Austen's sent her a story inviting her criticism, she replied:

You are now collecting your people delightfully, getting them exactly into such a spot as is the delight of my life; three or four families in a country village is the very thing to work on.

This statement admirably defines her own style and focus. She 'works on' her characters, embedding them in a clear language which reflects their class, position, refinement, vulgarity, weakness, moral code etc. Jane Austen does not stray outside the limits of her own experience, and that experience is of the small community with its intricacies and intrigues of personal relationships drawn on her 'small square, two inches, of ivory'. Life is not exciting or adventurous, in fact it is the relatively static life of the upper middle class and representatives of the English country gentry. Jane Austen is bound by their social conventions, and the language she uses conveys this.

Jane Austen has a great understanding of her own sex, and Emma is seen from the inside. Much of the novel is concerned with the revelations of Emma's consciousness – her ideas, whims, speculations, moments of grief or of exultation, as when she reacts to Knightley's proposal. Consequently the style of the novel exists on three distinct levels: the dialogue, which shows character in action; the inward consciousness of character; the authorial commentary on character, situation or even description. The tone is always eminently civilized and refined; there are strong emotions but they are expressed, so to speak, at a subdued pitch. The author's tone is basically an ironic one, so that we smile with her at the foibles and failings of, for example, Emma in her misreading of characters and situations. Each of the misunderstandings caused by Emma's love of match-making is so skilfully woven into the others that at no time does the plot lose its sense of reality.

Emma is a satire of vanity and self-deception as reflected in the character of Emma herself. Yet the tone is not overtly moral; the Jane Austen corrective is to employ humour to underline the misconceptions of her own heroine. More than that, humour, open and subtle, is found on nearly every page of the novel. We do not only think of Emma in this connection – we think of the plaintive and anxious Mr Woodhouse and his attention to his own and other people's diets; of Mrs Elton's snobbery; of Miss Bates's verbal stream. The humour throughout is delightful. Miss Bates's language is real – observed and heard with accuracy – and although on the surface she appears to be a caricature there is more to it than that. She is quite simply a bore but her long, disconnected monologues are entertaining to the reader. Her phrases are monotonous, but consider Emma's mimicry of her when she, Emma, disagrees with the possibility of Knightley's marrying Jane Fairfax. She speaks of him as being haunted all day by her aunt, Miss Bates, with her 'So very kind and obliging!' Emma goes on to define Miss Bates's irrelevancies by saying that she would then 'fly off, through half a sentence, to her mother's old petticoat – . Not that it was such a very old petticoat either – for still it would last a great while – and, indeed, she must thankfully say that their petticoats were all very strong.' Jane Austen's 'ear' is never at fault.

Mr Woodhouse, like Miss Bates, is also seen satirically, perhaps nowhere better than in his comments on Emma's portrait of Harriet: 'The only thing I do not thoroughly like is, that she seems to be sitting out of doors, with only a little shawl over her shoulders – and it makes me think she must catch cold.' Here the humour plays on the obsession, and we should note that Jane Austen's characters possess a kind of psychological truth, which is found in what they say and their manner of saying it. We all know a Mr Woodhouse; he is no caricature; in fact he exemplifies the art of realism.

There are many amusing comments on human nature in *Emma*. Emma's happy statement 'There does seem to be something in the air of Hartfield which gives love exactly the right direction, and sends it into the very channel where it ought to flow' is an ironic prelude to love flowing in every direction but the right one for her. Irony, often dramatic, is present throughout; we note it in Mr Elton's courtship of Emma which she thinks – as does poor Harriet – is a courting of Harriet. The same applies when Emma believes that Frank Churchill is in love with her, when all the time he is engaged to Jane Fairfax. Such irony reaches its height during the discussion between Frank and Emma about the origin of the gift of the piano. There is irony too in Emma's unwitting encouragement of Harriet's 'love' for Knightley (whom she comes to find that she herself loves), thinking all the time that she is fostering Harriet's hopes of securing Frank Churchill. The portrait of Emma herself, particularly in the early stages of the novel, is an ironic one; it is only when she comes to a greater degree of self-awareness that the tone and most of the comments change.

We are aware throughout of a kind of witty tone as well. Of course it is linked to the irony and the balance that are the hallmarks of Jane Austen's style. Take the impact of the following authorial comment on our appraisal of Emma's character – 'Something occurred while they were at Hartfield, to make Emma want their advice; and, which was still more lucky, she wanted exactly the advice they gave.' In encapsulated form here we have Emma's character; doing what she wants to do though needing advice to buttress her decisions. There is from time to time a lovely acidic quality about Jane Austen's observations. Take the following:

When lovely woman stoops to folly, she has nothing to do but die; and when she stoops to be disagreeable, it is equally to be recommended as a clearer of ill-fame.

Here Jane Austen takes Goldsmith's original words and turns them neatly into an epigram of her own. She half-quotes occasionally by way of illustration, but hers is not a heavy literary style. Its terseness is, however, often epigrammatic, as when Emma thinks to herself, 'For Mrs Weston there was nothing to be done; for Harriet, every thing.' This is typical of the polish of Jane Austen's style, seen at its best in the opening of Chapter 9 where once again insight and epigram cohere economically to produce the perfect statement that 'Mr Knightley might quarrel with her, but Emma could not quarrel with herself.'

The foregoing sections have indicated the main qualities of Jane Austen's style. There is a remarkable fluency, which carries the narrative forward, but it is the fluency that comes from art not chance (to adopt Pope's words), in Jane Austen's manner. The ease of expression, the balance, the exact choice of word, occasionally an equally exact choice of image, these are evident in *Emma*. We have said that the dialogue is natural, and it is true to say that Jane Austen's descriptions are natural too. Take the description of the Abbey and the Abbey-mill farm, where the exactness of the perspective is mirrored by the exactness of the prose. It is almost a landscape in words. But Jane Austen's best descriptions are of the interactions of people, and this is the genuine stuff of the novelist. Her blend of commentary and dialogue combines rational and moral appraisal on the one hand with psychological insight on the other. And when this is put in such a way as to embrace a variety of tones – satirical, ironic, conversational, witty, pathetic and others – we are aware that

Jane Austen's style is of its time but also for all time. The range appears narrow, but it is only as narrow as people. And people, as we know, are creatures of habit, suddenness, predictability, change, boredom, inspiration, whim. All these are Jane Austen's range, and the lucidity of her style enhances and individualizes the characters she creates.

General questions

1 In what ways does Jane Austen present Emma ironically?

Guideline notes which might be included in your answer:

(i) *Introduction* – Emma and her situation, her relationship with her father, the loss of Miss Taylor, her status in Highbury, reference to her married sister, Mr Knightley etc.

(ii) *Irony* in Chapter 1 about Emma's character – spoiled, used to having her own way, somewhat self-willed; failure to see anything through; awareness of status; snobbery (re Robert Martin); in fact, any points you can glean from the early chapters that are critical of Emma's conduct and attitudes.

(iii) *Main ironies* (be selective, for the ironic treatment of Emma runs the whole length of the novel). Emma and match-making re Harriet and Mr Elton; Emma misreading Elton's intentions (the framing of the portrait); Emma contriving to leave Harriet and Elton together; Emma watching Elton's interest in Harriet's illness which is really his fear that she (Emma) will catch it; leading to Emma trapped in the carriage and having to listen to Elton's proposal.

(iv) In roughly the same detail as above, Emma and her relationship with Frank Churchill and her imagining him in love with her when all the time he is interested in Jane Fairfax. Plenty of selective detail here, including the pianoforte, Mr Dixon etc.

(v) Emma and the mistake re Harriet and Frank, her encouraging Harriet re Knightley when she thinks Harriet is grateful to Frank. Continue other examples leading to her feeling that Knightley means to tell her that he is interested in Harriet, with all righted by his proposal.

(vi) *Conclusion* – Emma seen ironically throughout. Unusual stance for author to take towards her heroine, but provides wit, observation, psychological insight into the heroine while she is in the process of development and learning from experience. Author and reader both exercising a kind of moral judgement on Emma as she is seen in action. Only an ironic appraisal can provide for this.

2 In what ways do you get a distinct sense of *place* in *Emma*? You should refer closely to Highbury and the community in your answer.

3 To what extent are the involved situations in the novel caused by Emma's interfering nature?

4 Although Emma is spoiled, write an essay in defence of her and her actions. Refer closely to the text in support of your views.

5 In what ways do you consider Harriet Smith shallow? Write a reasoned account of her character based on evidence in the novel.

6 Write a character-study of Mr Knightley. Do you feel that he is all strength and good sense without weakness? Give reasons for your answer.

7 In what ways do you feel Jane Fairfax brings upon herself the sufferings that undermine her in Highbury? Again, you should refer closely to the text in your answer.

8 'Thoroughly selfish.' Is this an adequate or fair definition of the character of Frank Churchill?

9 'They certainly deserve each other.' Say whether you agree or disagree with this statement about Mr and Mrs Elton.

10 Write an essay on the *humour* in Emma, with particular reference to Mr Woodhouse and Miss Bates.

11 Write an essay on the chief aspects of Jane Austen's style, providing examples to qualify your statements.

12 Compare and contrast Mr and Mrs Weston *and* Mr and Mrs John Knightley.

13 'The tone may be light, but the morality is stern.' How far would you agree with this judgement of *Emma*?

14 Examine the quality of the dialogue in *Emma*. Do you consider that it is true to life?

15 Write an essay on Jane Austen's use of the unexpected in *Emma*.

16 In what ways is dramatic irony used in *Emma*?

17 'It is too limited an area for depth study.' How far would you agree or disagree with this assessment of *Emma*?

18 'Nothing much happens. It is all very trivial and unexciting.' How far do you agree with this comment on the novel?

19 Compare and contrast the visit to Donwell Abbey with the visit to Box Hill.

20 Write about any aspect(s) of *Emma* that interest you, and which have not been covered by the questions above.

Further reading

Lord David Cecil, *A Portrait of Jane Austen* (Penguin, 1980).

Pinion, F. B., *A Jane Austen Companion* (Macmillan, 1973).

Jenkins, Elizabeth, *Jane Austen: A Biography* (Macdonald, 1956).

Gilley, Christopher, *A Preface to Jane Austen* (Longman, 1974).

Wright, Andrew, *Jane Austen's Novels: a study in Structure* (Chatto & Windus, 1961).

Hardy, Barbara, *A Reading of Jane Austen* (Athlone Press, 1979).

Craik, W. A., *Jane Austen: the Six Novels* (Methuen, 1965).

Mudrick, Marvin, *Jane Austen: irony as defence and discovery* (Princeton, 1952).